# What Others Are Saying…

In a Christian environment that majors on marketing and therapy, Kary Oberbrunner gives us a shot in the chops reminding us that discipleship is the heart of ministry. This book beautifully outlines the why and how of authentic discipleship.

**– Dr. Bill Brown, president, Cedarville University**

If you're thirsty for some God–drenched insights on authentic discipleship, Called is a great place to start. Dr. Oberbrunner is drinking from some deep wells.

**– Matt Green, editor, Ministry Today**

Kary's passion for discipleship is infectious. You can't read this book and not be convinced of a need you can personally fulfill within the Church.

**– Cara Davis, editorial director, RELEVANT Media Group**

If "follow me," are the most important words uttered by Jesus, then "How?" is certainly the most pressing question we wrestle to answer. Kary seeks to answer the "how?" through the "why?" toward the "now what?" He's honest, insightful, and a worthy journeyer with each of our pursuits toward responding to Jesus' most compelling call.

**–Steven Argue, executive director– Contextual Learning Center,**
**Grand Rapids Theological Seminary**

Kary addresses discipleship with conviction and passion; this is not a "three easy steps" book but rather a serious call to a biblical lifestyle.

**– Mike Calhoun, vice pres… h Ministries,**
**Word of Life Fell… ng the Limits,**
**…ent Ministry.**

D1017768

Dietrich Bonhoeffer's call to disc… call to come and die. Kary Oberbrunner's call to discip… …tion is a call to come and live. Ironically both have always been tru… …sive to grasp. Called fuses these invitations into one transforming whole and offers us a pathway forward toward a life worth living.

**– Rob Yackley, director of NieuCommunities, nieucommunities.org**

The secret is out. Praying a prayer, walking an aisle, and getting saved is not the end of God's plan for the believer. God has in view for each believer a unique set of purposes, plans, gifts and challenges. Kary Oberbrunner challenges us to fulfill this plan by moving beyond an event called "getting saved" to the process of discipleship that God has envisioned for each of us. This is a call to a thoughtful and comprehensive discipleship of Jesus Christ.

**– David R. Plaster, Th. D., vice president,**
**Grace College and Grace Theological Seminary**

This is my kind of book. One that tells me the truth about who I am and what on earth I'm called to be and do. But, let me warn you. Before reading it, fasten your seatbelt. This isn't a "feel good" book...it's a "transform your life from the inside out so you can turn your world upside down" book. Get ready to leave your safe little world and head into the jungle with Almighty God.

**– Dr. Tim Elmore, founder, GrowingLeaders.com**

With the well-written Called, Kary Oberbrunner joins the chorus of emerging voices who are challenging Christ-followers to dump the evangelical status quo in favor of radical, life-changing discipleship. Bravo!

**– Angie Ward, associate director, Innovative Church Community**

Oberbrunner has the pulse of the current generation combined with God's plan for the ages to re–calibrate leadership training for the twenty first century.

**– Dr. Gene Heacock, executive director, Sandberg Leadership Center**
**Ashland Theological Seminary**

There is an easy, captivating style in Kary's writing so that almost unknowingly the reader will engage in deep, stimulating thought about what it means to be an authentic disciple of Jesus. The book does not permit neutrality, nor will the reader be able to slip quietly back into a comfortable "business as usual" approach to faith. This is a much-needed, practical call to exciting, incarnational Christianity.

**– Dr. Bill Rudd, pastor, Calvary Church, Fruitport, Michigan**

With a wisdom born of experience and a passion surging from a good man, Kary Oberbrunner speaks to our souls and urges us to embrace the call to "become who we were born to be."

**– Tammy Schultz, Ph.D., LMHC, chair, Graduate School in**
**Counseling and Interpersonal Relations, Grace College**

*A practical work reminding us of the serious call to, and work of, discipleship. This book gives the reader a theological, biblical, and practical understanding of becoming the disciples we were born to be.*

**– Dr. Leroy A. Solomon, doctor of ministry dean,**
**Ashland Theological Seminary**

*I highly recommend this book. Kary's passion to help others understand the breadth and depth of what it means to follow Jesus is infectious. This book offers an insightful exploration of what it means to be a disciple of Jesus. It is written in the spirit of Bonhoeffer's* Cost of Discipleship *with much needed practical examples for today's generation. Whether you are helping others become faithful followers of Jesus Christ or feel a need in your own life to live out your faith with integrity, this book is a valuable companion on the journey of becoming who you were born to be.*

**– Howard D. Van Cleave, associate national director,**
**InterVarsity Faculty Ministry**

*Kary challenges his readers to live out loud. He inspires us to question, doubt, embrace, and own our faith. Should we choose to rise to the occasion, we will find a fresh infusion of the living, active and powerful God. Read on and get ready for an adventure!*

**– Anne Thompson, Awake Entertainment**

*Too often the church seems more like a collection of body parts than a living and functioning organism. True discipleship must identify and unleash the church's mid-level leaders—the joints and ligaments that hold it together and allow it to fulfill its mission. Kary Oberbrunner's outstanding work is a major contribution toward reducing the gap between the professional ministry and the so-called laypeople.*

**– Dr. Tom Julien, executive director emeritus,**
**Grace Brethren International Missions**

*The next building block after* The Journey Towards Relevance. *Passionate, challenging, thought provoking, and informative. Kary's easy-to-read writing style makes this a book for everyone.*

**–Brett Ullman, director, Worlds Apart**

*There is only one way to discover the real you, and that is to become a disciple of Jesus Christ.* Called *will show you how to become the person you were meant to be.*

**– Harvey A. Hook, author of *The Power of an Ordinary Life***
**Executive Director, The Gathering, Columbus**

*If you desire the passionate Christian life, sense the urge to follow a bigger Jesus, one who requires more rather than less, then you will hearken to the call and do well to read this book along the way!*

**–Tim Boal, author of *Building Authentic Community*, executive director, Grace Brethren North American Missions**

*In the last 20 years we've relied on events, curriculum, and mass media to bring about spiritual transformation in America's youth. These techniques have their place, but they've never discipled anyone, and the hoped-for spiritual transformation has not materialized. Contrast that with the life of Christ. In three years of earthly ministry He trained twelve ordinary men to change the world. . . and they did it. This book gives you the tools you need to walk with others the way Jesus walked with His disciples. Experience the radical blessing that comes with doing God's thing God's way.*

**– Jeff Myers, Ph.D., president, Passing the Baton International, Inc.**

*This book reads like a discipleship manifesto for emerging leaders, bridging the gap between academia and real life. It's more than a book on discipleship, though; it's a provocative call to re-learn what it means to follow Christ with our minds and our hearts.*

**– Brian Orme, pastor, freelance religion writer for *Dayton Daily News***

*Dr. Kary Oberbrunner has done it again with this one, championing the idea that there is more to this faith we call Christianity than simply right belief and right behavior. Too many people are turned off by Christianity because all they see is an empty faith guided by rules and regulations instead of a loving and living God.* Called *shows how this faith is one where "no theological robots are allowed," and challenges the church to take a closer look at the Great Commission.*

**– Blair Halver, founder, Rebel Brand Clothiers**

*In his excellent new book* Called, *Dr. Kary Oberbrunner lovingly, yet firmly compels the church to re-evaluate discipleship, a crucial component of the Great Commission, on practical, as well as theological realms. Oberbrunner demolishes barricades to discipleship without ever lowering the bar. Accessible, but never simplistic,* Called *is an indispensable resource for pastors, teachers, leaders, and students alike.*

**– John McCollum, co–founder, Asia's Hope**

*A must read for anyone interested in truly understanding Jesus' heart concerning the committed Christian disciple.*

**– Marc Eckel, Splat Experience performance artist**

*"Will you become who you were born to be?" With this poignant question, Oberbrunner launches into a theme that has become his passion: believers not just surviving spiritual infancy, but thriving in their life-long pursuit of becoming all they were born to be in Christ. If you are sensing that the Jesus taught by many today is a watered-down Jesus who asks too little, the message of this book and its fresh look at the Jesus of the Bible will be a welcome read.*

**– Barb Wooler, missionary to Bayaka Pygmy people**

Called *provides an insightful, refreshing, and challenging look into what it means to be a true follower of Christ today. Kary reminds us that we must take the Lord's mandate to heart: to be and to make disciples, thus fulfilling the Great Commission!*

**– Nick C. Corrova, Campus Crusade for Christ International**

Called *will challenge you and guide you through the first steps of becoming the Christian leader God has called you to be. It is a powerful asset for pastors, lay leaders, youth leaders, and believers at all stages on their journey to becoming a disciple with a purpose. Dr. Kary Oberbrunner's style of writing is very open and his words speak to me like a pastor, mentor, and friend. I am encouraged as well as challenged to follow his teachings, which I firmly believe to be inspired by a genuine desire to follow God, and his desire to be a committed leader of God's flock.*

**– Ken Wiegman, AlphaOmegaNews.org**

Called *makes a lucid and compelling case for renewing our focus on discipleship. Kary has created a practical, balanced paradigm that helps us understand discipleship and its critical role in the life of faith today.*

**– Justin Baeder, church planter, RadicalCongruency.com**

# Called

## becoming who you were born to be

Kary Oberbrunner

**Called: becoming who you were born to be**

Copyright ©2007 by Kary Oberbrunner
BMH Books, P.O. Box 544
Winona Lake, Indiana 46590
www.bmhbooks.com

ISBN 10: 0-88469-087-3
ISBN 13: 978-0-88469-087-0
Christian Living/Practical Life/Personal Growth
CLV/CLF/PGR

All rights reserved. Written permission must be secured from the publisher to use or reproduce any part of this book, except for brief quotations in critical reviews or articles.

Unless otherwise noted, all Scripture quotations are taken from the New American Standard Bible®, Copyright © 1960, 1962, 1963, 1968, 1971, 1972, 1973,1975, 1977, 1995 by The Lockman Foundation. Used by permission. (www.Lockman.org)

Scripture quotations marked (NIV) are taken from the HOLY BIBLE, NEW INTERNATIONAL VERSION®. NIV®. Copyright©1973, 1978, 1984 by International Bible Society. Used by permission of Zondervan. All rights reserved.

Scripture quotations noted KJV are from The Holy Bible, KING JAMES VERSION.

Please note: The author has prepared the *CALLED* Workbook, a study guide to accompany this text. A description of the workbook will be found following the endnotes in this book.

Cover design by Brian Rants and Matt Brozovich eye9design.com

Printed in the United States of America

**for Keegan**

my "little fire"

May you realize the great purpose to which you have been called.

# ACKNOWLEDGEMENTS

The paradigm introduced in this book began haunting me years ago. What you hold in your hands is representative of its evolution. It was born out of the paralysis I felt when I learned about someone's conversion. Even as a pastor, I didn't know how to proceed.

I'm a pretty simple guy. I think in word pictures. Until that point in time, I didn't have a picture of the discipleship process. That has changed. If this book sheds a little light on the subject for you, if it clears up some of the mystery, then I'll be a happy camper.

This paradigm has been tested. You will find out more about that in the Afterword. The paradigm was also the substance of my doctoral dissertation. If you desire to obtain a copy of it, refer to my website (karyoberbrunner.com). You'll find more information there.

I want to thank some important people who provided me with significant feedback regarding this paradigm. Their input has made the philosophy, methodology, and reality of this paradigm stronger.

First, I thank my wife Kelly. She trusted my heart enough to give me the time to write.

I thank my church, the Grace Brethren Church of Powell and, specifically, Pastor Rick Nuzum. They believed in this paradigm enough to partner with me in the creation of it. Thanks to

Pastor Ed Jackson for his prayer and financial support in my doctoral program. Dr. Dave Plaster and Pastor Jeff Martin are two irreplaceable people who served on my D.Min. committee.

I am grateful, also, to my colleagues, Dustin Godshall, Dave Coleman, Sean Spoelstra, Phil Stoll, Tim Farner, and Mark Artrip for their encouragement.

Thanks to those brothers who take care of my soul and love me unconditionally: John Ward, Nate Harrison, Matt Reid, Mike Myers, Brian Rants, Abram Silvey, and Gary Underwood.

The DRIVEN steering committee: Keith Minier, Ezra Wimberly, and Mike Jentes have been a great encouragement to me. Thanks to John McCollum for believing and investing in the dreams within my heart and to my faithful first-draft editor Kylie Henretta. Thanks to Kate Ward with Draw productions and her desire for excellence in all she does. I am deeply indebted to Terry White and Jesse Deloe and BMH for their faith in this project.

I want to thank the panel of experts who took the time and effort to critique my dissertation, the theological and philosophical backbone of *Called*: Jeff Gill, Gary Webb, Ron Smals, Tony Webb, Roger Peugh, Mark Soto, Tim Waggoner, Larry Chamberlain, Wayne Hannah, Jason Carmean, Tim Boal, Dan Allan, Todd Scoles, Dave Bogue, Scott Feather, John Teevan, Blaine Horst, Clancy Cruise, Tom Julien, Tom Avey, Ken Bickel, Tom Stallter, Randy Smith, Tim Ruesch, Chip Heim, and Ryan Egli.

To the teens in the summer of 2006 Grace Institute, you guys are my inspiration. And to my U2 buddies Josh Grisdale and Luke Chaney, Cleveland was a good oasis amidst my time in the desert.

— Kary Oberbrunner<br>Powell, Ohio<br>November 2006

# FOREWORD

**"Called"** is a word that in the context of today's Christianity can sometimes be misunderstood and even misused by well-intended people. It's easy to think of *professional* Christians, those in full-time vocational ministry, as the only ones who have been called by God. This could not be further from the truth.

The fact is that we have all been called. When Christ called the disciples He was not asking them to take on a title but to take on a life, a new life that would be transformed by His teachings…a life that would show others this amazing transformation from selfish living to selfless living…a life that would be lived with eternity in mind and not simply the here and now.

And if we've been called, we've also been encouraged to "call others." When Christ addressed the disciples in Matthew 28, He charged them to make disciples. He told them to baptize them into this new life and teach them to observe what He had shown them. And while there is no easy formula to ensure the results will always be positive, we have been left with a manual, God's Word, which gives us principles to live by.

As a Christian, our life is not a sprint but a relay. The track is eternal. The baton we hold in our hand has been passed to us and we must pass it faithfully to others. And while the culture around us would tell us life is about running, Kary Oberbrunner reminds us it's really about the pass. He gives us foundational practices that will help us pass the baton more effectively...practices developed from the principles Christ Himself left for us.

In *Called*, Kary gets to the heart of the life we are all called to live. Furthermore, he weaves personal life experiences with biblical examples to encourage us to live with a larger life in mind. *Called* will equip and empower you to become who you were born to be, the person Jesus Christ has called you to be.

— Dr. Gene A. Getz
President, Center for Church Renewal
Author of more than 60 books including *Measure of a Man*
Adjunct Professor, Dallas Theological Seminary

The Church exists for no other purpose but to draw men into Christ, to make them little Christs. If they are not doing that, all the cathedrals, clergy, missions, sermons, even the Bible itself, are simply a waste of time. God became man for no other purpose. It is doubtful, you know, whether the whole universe was created for any other purpose.

– C. S. Lewis in *Mere Christianity*

# TABLE OF CONTENTS

# INTRODUCTION

## Your Epic Awaits You

To tell you the truth, I can often lose perspective. I can get so caught up with the little things in life. Sometimes I put a lot of stock in what people think of me or how the latest project turns out. Maybe you too get consumed with the small things of life—what your friend is wearing, the neighbor's new car, or even what's for dinner. Maybe life is more than this. Maybe it's bigger…much bigger. Maybe life is an adventure of epic proportions. Maybe we've just swallowed the lie that life is about who we know, what we accumulate, and the *stuff* that defines us.

I was at a coffee shop one night with my buddy, Brian Rants. I was on a little trip out in Colorado just getting a breather from the busyness of life. Brian was talking about some pretty profound things that night. He was telling me, "You know, Satan wants to destroy us. Of course, he tries to kill us in the obvious ways. He tries to make us murderers and child molesters. But you know what? Satan also tries to destroy us in subtle ways. He tries to make us safe. He attempts to declaw us by convincing us that life is about playing it small."

Brian went on to quote Marianne Williamson's inspiring words. Many people remember these words because Nelson Mandela spoke them in his 1994 inaugural speech. His words have sparked courage in my own soul over the last couple of years.

> Our deepest fear is not that we are inadequate. Our deepest fear is that we are powerful beyond measure. It is our own light, not our darkness, that most frightens us. We ask ourselves, who am I to be brilliant, gorgeous, talented and fabulous? Actually, who are you not to be? You are a child of God. *Your playing small doesn't serve the world.* There's nothing enlightened about shrinking so that other people won't feel insecure around you. We were born to manifest the glory of God that is within us. It's not just in some of us; it's in everyone. And as we let our light shine, we unconsciously give other people permission to do the same. As we are liberated from our own fear, our presence automatically liberates others.[1]

Brian was right. Our enemy tries to kill us softly—to get us to doubt ourselves and live in fear, to get us so wrapped up in the insignificant stuff of life that we are declawed and about as fierce as a piece of wet cardboard. This book is not about wet cardboard. Instead, it reveals the false doctrine of discipleship that many of us have bought. It exposes the lie that says, *Accept Jesus into your heart and then go on your merry way and live the rest of your life, calling your own shots*. It debunks the myth that life is all about you and what you want.

Instead, this book proves that life is all about God. It demonstrates that authentic discipleship is more about dying than living. It describes a feeling that maybe you've always felt, but one that scares you to death. It suggests that you've been *called*.

Called? Called to what? Called to more than you know, more than you think, more than you can touch and taste and feel. Whether you realize it or not, you've been called to an adventure of epic proportions. You've been called to become who you were born to be.

For some reason, even though I grew up in the church, I never got this memo. Maybe I slept through the orientation or maybe I was just daydreaming. Either way, I missed it. Rest easy if you missed it too, THIS book is THAT memo.

# Part 1

# WHY DISCIPLESHIP?

# The Baby Factory

*Dream no small dreams for they have no power to move the hearts of men.*
Johann Wolfgang von Goethe

I never saw anything like it before. It's not every day that you get to witness a birth. Maybe you've never had the chance. It can be bloody. It's often joyous. Many times it's painful physically, emotionally, and even spiritually. Bringing a new life into the world is beyond words.

Witnessing one birth is unbelievable, but I'll never forget the day I saw 300 babies being born in a matter of 10 minutes. It sounds like a stretch, I know. I still can't believe it. Let's just say I didn't know what I was walking into. The celebration after the births was indescribable. People were cheering for five minutes straight.

It's difficult to get a room big enough for 300 babies to be born. The actual room we were in was built to hold about 3,500 people. The facility was updated with the latest technology. It would have to be with the expectation of that many births.

Many trained professionals were in the room that evening. The combined schooling of these professionals would make Sallie Mae (the nation's leading provider of student loans) salivate. Most of the births involved teenagers. Some teens entered the room scared; others seemed relaxed.

There were cameras all around. The seats for us spectators were incredibly comfortable. Still, we all felt tense. There was one main guy who was in charge. He was in his late sixties or early seventies. He was a prolific author and an expert in his field.

The evening started with a lot of excitement. When the expert stood up, we all hushed. Everyone knew something special was in the air. After about 45 minutes of explaining the details concerning the birth, the expert was ready.

At this point the tension rose slightly. People quieted down. Some began to pray. A few even started to cry. Then it happened. I couldn't believe it. I started to squirm in my chair. I didn't know quite what to do, so I just stared. I knew it wasn't polite to stare, but I couldn't help it.

The crowd started to clap. One by one, births from all over the room happened spontaneously. There were cheers. A woman shouted, "Thank you God!"

In a matter of about 10 minutes, the births were over. Strangely, I found myself a bit saddened. You might think this odd. After all, how many people get to witness an act of God of this magnitude in their lifetime? But I couldn't help it. My sadness soon became a mild depression.

I thought about the huge task it would be to care for these 300 babies. Who was going to do it? When one baby is born, it can be overwhelming. My wife and I feel blessed, but we're often exhausted when caring for our little boy Keegan. New babies wake you up in the middle of the night. You can't just leave them there by themselves.

Sadly though, I knew most of these new babies would be left to fend for themselves.

Yet, here I was the only realist in the group. I was raining on everyone else's parade. People were rejoicing, and I was stewing over the details. Sadly though, I knew most of these new babies would be left to fend for themselves. Although I wanted to hope for the best, I knew that when it came down to it, no one really had the time or know-how to raise all these babies. Who could really disciple all these brand new Christians?

## What Are We Doing?

Jesus never told us to *be* converts, much less *make* converts. He never told us to stay baby Christians or make baby Christians. His last words before He left this earth were, "Go therefore and make disciples of all the nations, baptizing them in the name of the Father and the Son and the Holy Spirit, teaching them to observe all that I commanded you; and lo, I am with you always, even to the end of the age."[1]

You know what's sad about that statement? Jesus tells us to make disciples, and many of us don't even know what a disciple is. Worse than that, we aren't sure if we *are* truly disciples. It's pretty hard to make something that you can't define.

*Jesus tells us to make disciples, and many of us don't even know what a disciple is.*

Maybe I'm being too negative. But try to define what a disciple is. That's the easiest part of the entire process. Next, explain how to measure authentic discipleship. (If you're going to make something, you need to be able to measure to see if it's authentic.) Finally, tell me the components that comprise discipleship.

I don't mean to sound like I have all the answers. I don't. I'm simply asking, what's wrong with the state of the church today? Do you know how hard it is to get Christians to even talk about discipleship? Something is wrong when the leaders of our churches can't define what a disciple is, explain how to determine the authenticity of a disciple, and list the components that make up real discipleship. I think we intentionally avoid the question.

Every church across the country, every campus ministry, every Christian school wants to make disciples. Why wouldn't they? That is why followers of Jesus were left on earth—to make more followers of Jesus. Yet, many of these same institutions can't verbalize the measurements and components that represent authentic discipleship, much less define what a disciple is.

Is there a biblical solution? Has Jesus left us clueless or do the pages of Scripture contain the answers? Is there a paradigm that cuts through the confusion?

## The Bare Minimum

In my experience, the extent of discipleship I've been presented with goes something like this:

1. Accept Jesus and ask Him into your heart.
2. Don't do bad things now.
3. Withdraw from culture.
4. Hang out with Christians.
5. Go to church.
6. Read your Bible and pray.
7. Be happy that you are saved and not going to hell.
8. Tell other people about how happy they can be if they follow those seven steps.

Is it just me, or is this a lame life? Where is the passion? Where is the adventure? Where is the abundant life that Jesus promised? No wonder we're bored. The Jesus we've been presented with asks for way too little. No one wants to devote his life to something that requires nothing of him. As the saying goes, "People figure, if it don't ask much, then it ain't worth much."

What about the Jesus who says something like this?

1. I want your whole life—everything—including your heart, soul, mind, and strength.[2]
2. I want to form myself in you.[3]
3. I want to transform you and then have you transform culture.[4]
4. I want you to be in the world as I was.[5]
5. I want you to be the church, the incarnation of me.[6]
6. I want you to embody the Word to others.
7. I am giving you abundant life now and will do so throughout eternity.[7]
8. Be my hands and feet in this world and see people as people, not projects to convert.

The reason why the world rejects Jesus is not because He asks too much. The Jesus we present asks too little. Jesus tells us that if we're going to be His disciples, we must be ready and willing to die.[8] Sounds like fun, doesn't it? No wonder few people want to talk about the cost of discipleship. No wonder there is so much confusion. Our understanding of discipleship has been watered down.

Many of us are caught up with our own agendas, desires, and plans. Why wouldn't we be? We've been told to accept Jesus. He comes to us. He knocks at the door of our hearts. He's waiting for us…isn't He?

*The reason why the world rejects Jesus is not because He asks too much. The Jesus we present asks too little.*

The Jesus I see in Scripture says, "Follow me." We don't put Jesus in our pocket as some kind of trinket that grants our wishes and wards off evil, bad weather, and police who pull us over for speeding. Discipleship is much larger, much grander.

Thanks to Kanye West we learned that "*Jesus Walks with Me*." As with his 2004 song, so went the need for following Jesus. The version of the music video I saw had Kanye leading the way with Jesus following him around. The Jesus in the video looked like a poor imitation of the plastic Burger King guy in those old TV commercials. He was aloof and detached, hardly a picture of the Son of God or Lord of lords. Has the call of Jesus been reduced to a pseudo allegiance of merely allowing Jesus to intersect our lives on rare occasions while following us as we lead the way?

Kanye is hardly to blame. I think we have bought into a new Jesus who allows us to live our lives any way we desire. Things rarely get difficult because Jesus never calls us to do anything. There is no following Him. He's the one who follows us. He's our personal genie who answers our every desire. He helps us win our fantasy football league or gives us the right answers on our final exams.

I've been in churches where you might think Jesus has some kind of codependent complex. It's as if He can't go on with life if we don't receive Him. We're made to feel guilty if we don't ask Him into our hearts. It's as if Jesus is in a pitiful state, sitting by the telephone waiting for us to call. He's made out to be a desperate reality show contestant who can't exist without us.

Where did we learn to view salvation like this? In the Scriptures I see a Jesus who says something like:

> Look, if you're not willing to count the cost ahead of time, then don't bother coming to me.[9]
>
> I love you beyond words, but you're going to have to carry a cross here. I'll help you carry it, but discipleship takes effort.[10]
>
> I'm not offering you a cheap ticket out of hell. It cost me everything and so I want all of you. It's free for you, but in a way it will cost you everything. I'm offering you abundant life, here and now, and for all eternity. But you're going to have to die to yourself every day.

Jesus has great compassion. He cares for us and loves us so much. But we do Christianity no favor by lowering the bar on discipleship. When we present an accommodating, no-commitment version of discipleship, we're altering the gospel. That is part of the reason that there is so much confusion about discipleship. Discipleship is *the* reason why we're left on earth. Discipleship is *the* crux of the Great Commission. And discipleship is *the* issue perplexing the church today.

It's time we return to a biblical understanding of what it means to be an authentic disciple.

I believe there are a few out there willing to cut through the confusion. Jesus said, "Many are called, but few are chosen."[11] Maybe you're one of those "few." Are you willing to fulfill the Great Commission and make disciples? If you're not sure you're a disciple, are you willing to explore what it means truly to be one? It's time we return to a biblical understanding of what it means to be an authentic disciple. Somehow it seems as though its meaning has been lost along the way. And strangely, it seems as though many of us have gotten lost along the way as well.

> Unfortunately, few Christians seem to understand what this (The Great Commission) means, at least when it comes to daily living. Even persons who are in leadership positions of the church have no idea how to go about teaching others to observe all things that Jesus commanded.
>
> Leroy Ei

# The Larger Story

*When it is time to die, let us not discover that we never lived.*
Henry David Thoreau

I dare you to try something. It is odd, but please hear me out. Go to your local video rental store. Pick out a movie you have never seen before. It doesn't really matter what genre it is, as long as you've never seen it before. Don't even read the description on the back and don't get a movie your friend has told you about. Just get one with a rating you're comfortable with.

Pop that DVD in the player and select from the menu a scene somewhere in the middle of the movie. Watch the movie for about 10 minutes and then turn it off.

What was your experience? Was it difficult to make sense of the plot? Did you understand the underlying direction of the movie?

Most likely, you were confused. Things probably seemed random and detached, and you felt like you had to add personal interpretation to fill in some of the blanks. Without any concept of the struggle or larger story at hand, you might have felt lost. You probably were able to see a smaller story within the larger story, and that smaller story made some sense. Yet, how that smaller story ties into the larger story is anyone's guess.

## The Small Story

Sadly, this is how most of us see our lives. We often feel that things are random and detached. We add our own interpretation in order to make sense of things. It's tough for us to see where things are going because we can't see what God is doing behind the scenes.

> *Sadly, this is how most of us see our lives. We often feel that things are random and detached.*

Many times we have the same experience when reading the Bible. Nobody reads the Bible in one sitting, so most likely, we pop open the Bible and flip through a few pages. We read a couple of paragraphs. Maybe a few of us actually digest an entire book of the Bible in one sitting.

Still, what's the result? Just like the movie challenge above, we grasp only a small story. This smaller story usually makes sense, but unless we have a concept of the larger story, we can't really get our hands around the ultimate underlying theme. We know that all Scripture is profitable, but many of us get lost in the Bible and in our own lives because we don't see God's larger story.

## The Larger Story

God is writing a larger story. He intends each of us to play a role in that larger story. We first have to know what that story is all about. Then we have to choose to become part of the story. The story line isn't something we have to guess about. The Creator has always intended that His godly seed be spread throughout the earth. Beginning in Genesis and ending in Revelation, the idea of discipleship, illustrated in the "Story of the Seed," saturates the Scriptures. (See the "Appendix.")

It was to this end that we were created. Most theologians would contend, according to the *Westminster Confession of Faith*, our chief purpose is to glorify God and enjoy Him forever.[1] Although I'd agree with this, according to Isaiah 43:7, my question is, how? How do we ensure that we glorify God and enjoy Him forever?

I believe that discipleship is inherently linked with achieving this purpose. I would say that discipleship is *the* way we glorify God and enjoy Him forever. Jesus said, "My Father is glorified in this, that you bear much fruit, and so prove to be My disciples."[2] In other words, the way we glorify God is by bearing fruit, and bearing that good fruit is proof that we are His disciples. Disciples are truly the only ones who can bear good fruit. We also know from Scripture that Jesus is preparing a place for us. Only those who are His disciples will be with Him forever and enjoy Him forever. Discipleship, therefore, is the only means to glorify God and enjoy Him forever.

God's first command to His original creation (Adam and Eve) and Jesus' last command to His new creation (the church) are very similar. Both offer an exhortation to spread godly seed throughout the earth. As one looks closer, the commands are extremely similar in both form and function.

> *And God said to them, "Be fruitful and multiply,*
> *and fill the earth..."*
>
> Genesis 1:28a

> *And Jesus spoke to them, "Go therefore and make disciples*
> *of all the nations..."*
>
> Matthew 28:18a, 19a

Created in the image of God, Adam and Eve were commanded to reproduce and fill the earth. Regenerated with a new nature, the disciples were commissioned to reproduce and fill the earth. The Great Commission in Matthew is a restatement of God's original desire and command to Adam and Eve in Genesis.

God's larger story is that we are to be His disciples and make other disciples. Until we acknowledge this truth and abandon our smaller story, becoming part of His larger story, our lives will never make sense, nor will they be fulfilling. Sadly, most of us never catch this larger story. Instead, we busy ourselves with our own small stories. We care

*Most of us never catch this larger story. Instead, we busy ourselves with our own small stories.*

more about whom we'll marry, how our careers will turn out, and whether or not our team is in the Super Bowl. Such things might seem important, but they pale against the backdrop of God's larger story. If we fail to recognize His story, our lives will never make sense.

It's quite the opposite if we recognize that God is writing a larger story. If we submit our smaller story to Him, our lives will have purpose and meaning. A person can't just muster up a desire for discipleship on his or her own. Rather, as we catch the larger story, we'll understand the wisdom, glory, and brilliance of our God. His story is truly amazing, and if we grasp the significance of it, my guess is that we'll want to be part of it.

We need to recognize our role in God's larger story. If we fail to realize the main plot, we will fail to see our role in it. C. S. Lewis believed that the church and believers are called to no higher purpose than discipleship.

> The Church exists for no other purpose but to draw men into Christ, to make them little Christs. If they are not doing that, all the cathedrals, clergy, missions, sermons, even the Bible itself, are simply a waste of time. God became man for no other purpose. It is doubtful, you know, whether the whole universe was created for any other purpose.[3]

In Jesus' short ministry here on earth, He spent most of His time making disciples. He could have done a lot of things, but He chose to invest His time in a few people. God has always been passionate about the spreading of His seed throughout the earth. He desires that the whole earth be filled with His knowledge and glory. "For the earth will be filled with the knowledge of the glory of the Lord, as the waters cover the sea."[4] He didn't commission the church to make converts, but rather disciples.

We have a choice. Each one of us has a smaller story. We have desires and goals. We have hopes and dreams. But that smaller story prevents us from playing a role in God's larger story if we're unwilling to submit it to Him. God's goal isn't to squash our dreams or desires. Yet we must put everything in check by first submitting our whole selves to Him.

We must ask ourselves if we're willing to entrust our small story to God, believing that being part of His larger story has a much greater reward. I don't think there is anything unspiritual in asking God, "What's in it for me?" Peter did. I'm glad Peter was real enough to ask Jesus this question. Perhaps part of the reason we have heard the gospel is that people like Peter abandoned their smaller stories to be part of God's larger story. Peter chose to respond to the call and be an authentic disciple. Have you?

> *Peter began to say to Him, "Behold, we have left everything and followed You."*
>
> *Jesus said, "Truly I say to you, there is no one who has left house or brothers or sisters or mother or father or children or farms, for My sake and for the gospel's sake, but that he shall receive a hundred times as much now in the present age, houses and brothers and sisters and mothers and children and farms, along with persecutions; and in the age to come, eternal life. But many who are first, will be last, and the last, first."*
>
> Mark 10:28-31

# Part 2

# HOW IS DISCIPLESHIP MEASURED?

# The Call

*Our mistake lies not in the intensity of our desire for happiness, but in the weakness of it.*
John Piper

Who wouldn't want to participate in "Job Shadow Day" some time during her high school career? All it took to convince me were two words: "No homework." Job Shadow Day is fairly simple. All you have to do is pick a career, tell the school, and have them pair you up with someone to follow around all day. The wise thing is to follow someone in a profession that interests you. That's the purpose after all, to learn more about the ins and outs of a potential career.

I decided to go for the gold. I told the guidance counselor I wanted to be a cop. As a result, I'd get the opportunity to ride around in a police car all day and make arrests, or so I thought. As country star Keith Urban sings, "Who wouldn't want to be me?"

The day turned out better than I could ever have imagined. Prior to my Job Shadow Day, I received a call from Officer Dave. I was a little giddy, to say the least, about receiving the call. We set up the details for the upcoming day.

When the day finally came, I was beside myself. Officer Dave told me exciting tales while I sat shotgun in his cruiser. He let me carry his billy club. This billy club was not one of the old school wooden ones. No. This was more like a nightstick. It was about seven inches long. With one flick of the wrist, it extended into a pretty convincing weapon. As a sophomore in high school, I felt like I was on top of the world that day. It's a wonder I didn't become a cop.

Officer Dave took me on a tour of the police station. He typed in a code on a keypad to open the garage where all of the cruisers were parked. I remember trying to sneak a peek at the code just in case I'd ever need that important information. You never know when you and your teenage buddies might need the password to a police garage.

Yeah, it was quite an interesting day. We even busted a guy for urinating on a lawn in public. I stuck to Officer Dave like glue because I didn't want to miss a thing. Besides, I had confidence that he knew the ropes. I didn't want to get into trouble. I assumed every day on the police force was like the *COPS* TV show. Even though our day wasn't as crazy as *COPS*, it would have been foolish not to follow Officer Dave. If I had led him around, it would have defeated the purpose of Job Shadow Day. In order to have the adventure that I did, I had to leave my routine at the high school and step out into the unknown. I had to put my trust in Officer Dave, follow him, and believe that he had my best interest in mind.

## Shadowing Jesus

Discipleship is no different. Jesus gives us a call. He presents us with an adventure. Prior to embarking, we first need to abandon our routine. We can't go with God and stay with self. We must step out into the unknown with Jesus. We must put our trust in Him, follow Him, and believe that He has our best interest in mind.

Just as I had to follow Officer Dave to have a purposeful and eventful experience, we need to follow Jesus in the same manner. Jesus wants to show us some pretty amazing things as well. He wants to have an intimate relationship with us so that we experience Him daily.

I think we sometimes complicate discipleship. The Greek word for disciple (*mathētēs*) is simply translated "a follower." Thus, a disciple of Christ is a follower of Christ. If we want to be good disciples of Jesus, then we need to be good followers of Jesus. It's pretty simple, but it takes true humility.

We all know the notorious story about the guy who refuses to stop and ask for directions. We can guess why such a person refuses. Maybe it's because he's embarrassed to admit he's lost. Maybe he's too proud to ask for help. Maybe it's because he feels that stopping will slow him down and make him lose more time. Regardless, only a teachable and humble person can admit he needs help.

Sadly, much of our world is too self-sufficient to admit its dependence. Instead, we're taught from a very young age to be independent. We're told to be our own person and provide for ourselves. Regarding salvation, this advice is about as foolish as my trying to lead Officer Dave around on Job Shadow Day. It defeats the purpose. We dare not have Jesus follow us around. Rather, a true disciple is one who follows Jesus. The first step in following is to answer the call.

## Don't Forget the Magic Words

Two words can change your life. Two words have changed many people's lives. "I do" have been the defining words that have altered the way many people face their lives on a daily basis. These two words, often uttered at church altars, signify a lifetime commitment cemented by God that no person should put asunder. These two words represent the beginning of a permanent relationship in which separate individuals become one flesh. I don't know of any two words more powerful—except for two other words.

Jesus often utters two other words. They would not be nearly so powerful as "I do," except for the fact that it is Jesus who speaks them. When the Son of God comes to you and says, "Follow Me," time stands still for a few moments. I think even the angels hang on the edge of their seats, eager to see how you'll respond.

Jesus doesn't have to know someone long before offering the call of discipleship. For some individuals, these are the very first words He ever speaks to them.[1] Forget standard greetings. Jesus gets right to the point. He presents people with a fairly cut-and-dried choice. Will they follow Him or will they blow Him off? There is no middle ground. With Jesus there is never any middle ground.

Jesus isn't impressed with people who *seem* sincere about following Him. One time someone came to Jesus while He was in a big crowd. This guy said he would follow Jesus wherever He went. You'd think Jesus would be pretty excited about this man's public commitment. The man was no slouch. He knew the Law. He was a tremendous asset. He was an educated man. This scribe said to Jesus, "Teacher, I will follow You wherever You go."[2]

In an incredibly public way, an exceedingly capable man made a bold commitment to Jesus. How did Jesus respond? After all, the scribe did utter the magic words. He did say he would follow Jesus wherever He went. This guy could have been a candidate for the Job Shadow Day poster child that you might see on high school lockers.

Instead, Jesus responded harshly. He said, "The foxes have holes and the birds of the air have nests, but the Son of Man has nowhere to lay His head."[3] Jesus saw into this man's heart. He knew the scribe would have a problem with the whole lodging gig that was part of following Him. This scribe wanted to follow Jesus as long as he had a roof over his head. He was putting comfort before following Jesus.

Jesus wasn't desperate to have this guy on His team. He didn't lower the bar on discipleship simply because the man wanted a pillow to sleep on at night. Instead, Jesus actually raised the bar of discipleship by publicly holding His ground. Jesus discouraged this guy from being a disciple. The scribe wasn't ready to follow Him. He didn't truly grasp what discipleship entailed. Instead of letting him off the hook, Jesus actually took it to him even harder.

*Jesus wasn't desperate to have this guy on His team. He didn't lower the bar on discipleship.*

One of Jesus' disciples who heard all this felt a bit uneasy. He said to Jesus, "Lord, permit me first to go and bury my father."[4]

Again, Jesus didn't miss a beat. He simply said, "Follow Me, and allow the dead to bury their own dead."[5] The disciple was referring to the Jewish obligation of taking care of one's parents. Most likely his father wasn't dead at that moment. Instead, he was stating the fact that before he could commit 100 percent, he would have to put certain things in order, like his father's burial plans. This man put competing commitments before Jesus.

Again, Jesus didn't lower the bar. He didn't dismiss him to do his tasks. This is contrary to the Jesus who has often been presented to us. The Jesus presented in many of our churches waits for us. He is a codependent king who lets us take care of our careers, our dreams, and our whims first and foremost. That is not the real Jesus. The real Jesus gives us quite a different call. He says to us, "If anyone wishes to come after Me, he must deny himself, and take up his cross daily and follow Me."[6] If we're going to follow Jesus, if we're really going to be His disciples, then it will take a daily practice of carrying our cross and dying to self.

How did people respond to Jesus when He raised the bar on discipleship in these two instances? Did they throw up their hands, believing that Jesus was a little over the top? After all, who really wants to follow someone that extreme? Shouldn't Jesus tame down His message a little? It seemed like He would lose people if He didn't cut them a little slack. But quite the opposite happened.

Sure Jesus lost some numbers because He didn't water down His message, but He probably lost the people who wouldn't have helped the ministry. There will always be "convenient Christians" who stick around because of the fringe benefits. Who wouldn't want a Messiah that pumps out free happy meals? Jesus didn't offer people this option though.

*Sure Jesus lost some numbers because He didn't water down His message, but He probably lost the people that wouldn't have helped the ministry.*

Jesus said it how it was, even if it meant losing potential followers. After all, true followers are those who follow Jesus, not the other way around. Raising the bar on discipleship brought a certain type of respect to the position. Those who followed Him realized it was not a game. They couldn't manipulate Him into becoming their personal genie. What was the result? How did those around Jesus respond to His harsh words? "When He got into the boat, His disciples followed Him."[7]

The true disciples became stronger in their commitment. They could have taken the easy way out in this situation. Remember, Scripture referred to that guy who wanted to bury his father as a "disciple." The other disciples could have opted out as well. Instead, they jumped in the boat with Jesus. They embodied the word disciple. They did what disciples do. They followed Jesus.

## Don't Let Your Nets Become Anchors

Early in the Gospels Jesus called the twelve disciples. These potential disciples weren't just sitting on the side of the road, twiddling their thumbs, waiting for an adventure to hit them upside the head. It's not as if Jesus wandered down the boardwalk and called a bunch of retired guys who had nothing better to do than play chess.

Jesus confronted some young men in the prime of their careers. They had everything going for them. These guys were tough. "Rough" was the adjective often used to describe people in such a profession.[8] They had a very prominent business that guaranteed them a healthy amount of job security. Their business had such great demand that cities often centered around the fruits of their labor.[9] These guys were fishermen.

One day two brothers, Simon and Andrew, were doing their usual fishing thing when Jesus arrived on the scene. He called them with the two powerful words: "Follow Me!"[10] Some guy they'd never seen before came up and told them, "Follow Me." They didn't ask Him who He was. They didn't ask Him where He was going. They simply received a call and had a few seconds to respond to it.

Jesus said, "I will make you fishers of men." I've always wondered what in the world that means. I don't know for sure. I don't think they knew at that time either. At best, He promised them a confusing alternative to fishing for fish. His guarantee of making them fishers of men wasn't all that attractive. They probably had no idea what it meant.

The words, "Immediately they left their nets and followed him," seem pretty trivial when separated from the emotion behind their actions.[11] For fishermen, their nets were a means of financial provision, security, familiarity, and identity. Some even had families to provide for. Peter later reiterated the fact that he and others left everything to follow Christ.[12] They didn't contemplate, rationalize, or introspect. When Christ called them, the disciples abandoned *good things* for a greater goal. Their nets (natural talents, means of financial gain, identity, significance) didn't become anchors, holding them back from moving into a deeper relationship with God.

*When Christ called them, the disciples abandoned good things for a greater goal.*

Still today, Jesus calls people to follow Him. Sadly, many of us simply just want a ticket out of hell. We want to skip over the "loving God with our whole self" part. In a symbolic sense, many Christians have allowed their nets (natural talents, identity, jobs, security) to become anchors, holding them back from a deeper knowledge of Christ. "Immediately" Peter, James, John, and Andrew released their nets, those good things God had given them, for a greater cause. They didn't let the cares of the world or desires for financial security weigh them down from following Jesus.

The call to discipleship wasn't an isolated event. When Jesus called Philip, He didn't even tell him about the fisher of men deal. He was even more obscure. Jesus didn't expound on what Philip could expect while following Him. He didn't tell him about the retirement benefits, the health insurance plan, or even where his next meal would come from. He simply said two words, "Follow Me."[13] And surprisingly, Philip did.

Matthew also responded promptly when Jesus called. Again Jesus simply said, "Follow Me."[14] Matthew was at his job. The nets he gave up were financial security, identity, and livelihood. Matthew may have given up earthly riches, but he gained heavenly reward. The first step was reckless abandonment. One can't go with God and stay with self.

*In our day, however, the Church has bought a lie at the other extreme.*

True discipleship doesn't mean heartless devotion and needless sacrifice. In our day, however, the church has bought a lie at the other extreme. We believe that Jesus is our personal genie. We think we can stay exactly where we are and still follow Jesus. If we're honest, many of us would much rather be the one leading Jesus around. Jesus doesn't present Himself this way. He wants us to follow Him immediately when He calls. We can't follow Him if we're letting things hold us back. When we do, we let our nets become anchors.

Hebrews 12:1 speaks about these "nets," which can be potentially positive. They aren't necessarily sinful habits, lifestyles, or activities. Discipleship not only demands the abandonment of sin, but also the good things that take precedence and priority over a love relationship with God. Paul even considered his righteousness, education, descent, and confidence as dung compared to knowing Christ.[15]

What are the nets in your life? In other words, what are those *good things* God has given you that crowd Him out of your heart? At times some of my "nets" have been relationships, dreams, and hobbies. Of themselves these things weren't bad or harmful. Most of them were tools God used eventually to deepen my relationship with Him. However, if left unchecked, the "nets" can quickly become the things "which so easily entangle" my heart. These nets can become *anchors* that weigh down my relationship with God.

We each have a choice. We have received a simple call. Two words never meant so much. "Follow Me" seems like a big sacrifice only when we look at what we're leaving. The disciples didn't look at what they were leaving. Instead they looked at who they were following. When they looked at Him, the things holding them back really didn't mean much.

I'm not saying we need to give up our houses, careers, and comforts to follow Jesus. For some of us we might. Remember though, Peter did go fishing later in his life.[16] It's not as if Jesus made him detest his hobbies and passions from then until eternity. However, there was a point when Peter needed to let go of everything. If he didn't, he never would have been able to follow Jesus. Sometimes Jesus gives back certain things that we give up for Him. That is His prerogative.

All I know is we can't play games. We can't hesitate once we've received the call. We must let go and follow Him. After all, that is the simple definition of a disciple, a follower.

# The Measurements

*Know thyself.*
Socrates

Somewhere along the way Christians learned it was wrong to be concerned about measuring up. Every believer seems to know this; it's part of our club rules. After all, grace is free, right? God will never love us any more or any less than He already does. Thankfully, His love is unconditional, and we can never add to or subtract from our salvation. This stuff is Christianity 101.

So why are we writing about measuring up? For starters the Bible commands us. "Test yourselves *to* see if you are in the faith; examine yourselves."[1] We dare not walk around measuring ourselves against other disciples. But we each must look to see how we're doing as disciples. I believe the Bible provides checks and balances to measure how we are doing as followers of Jesus.

I've put these checks and balances into a simple paradigm. In this chapter I'll give you a brief overview of the measurements. In the next few chapters we'll take an in-depth exploration of how those measurements affect our lives.

I like to think in pictures. So to humor me, flip to page 034 in order to familiarize yourself with the paradigm. Notice that it deals with how discipleship is measured. The paradigm is crucial because it forces us to look in the mirror. Not many people like to look in the mirror physically, or spiritually, for that matter.

Still, if we're going to understand what it means to follow Jesus authentically then we must get an accurate picture of where we are, so that we can effectively journey to where we must be. It may sound a bit heady at first, but it will be worth it.

The Bible's checks and balances examine all facets of being a follower of Jesus. This process holistically measures four areas. *Knowing*, related to epistemology; *being*, related to ontology; and *doing*, related to axiology, have everything to do with discipleship.[2] These three main subdivisions, often linked to the discipline of philosophy, are three of the four essential measurements of authentic discipleship. The fourth measurement of authentic discipleship is *reproducing*.

God has built into these subdivisions a natural system of checks and balances. Obviously, God is the supreme model for us in the three traditional subdivisions of philosophy: knowing, being, and doing. God is omniscient, all-knowing.[3] God is omnipresent, all-being.[4] God is omnipotent, all-doing.[5] The Creator who calls us to authentic discipleship in terms of our knowing, being, and doing is Himself all-knowing, all-being, and all-doing!

As examined in detail in chapter 2, the fourth and final measurement of authentic discipleship is reproducing. According to Matthew 28, all disciples have been commanded to reproduce other disciples. The spread of godly seed throughout the entire earth is on God's heart. God desires that disciples reproduce.

Knowing, being, doing, and reproducing are the four essential measurements of authentic discipleship. These four areas offer a holistic evaluation of the authenticity of a disciple.

On the surface it might not seem flashy or earth-shattering. That's what I thought until I studied the ramifications of these four measurements. Now my life is not the same as it was before.

Why are the measurements of discipleship so important? The Bible refers to Judas as a disciple.[6] Yet we know that he ended up betraying Jesus, hanging himself, and going to hell.[7] Judas didn't *lose* his salvation. He didn't fall away as an authentic disciple. I believe he never was one. Anyone could have known this if they had used the paradigm when looking at Judas' life.

But they didn't. So the Twelve were shocked when Jesus said one of His disciples would betray Him.[8] They didn't even believe Jesus when He revealed Judas as the betrayer.[9]

The point is that we all should be a little bit uneasy about how we measure up. I believe strongly in resting in our salvation. However, I'm afraid people too often trust in an event, rather than a person. Let me explain. Many people may have walked an aisle years ago and claimed a belief in Jesus Christ. Still, if there is no life change, if those disciples haven't moved off their couches to follow Jesus, they're no better off than the demons.[10] Remember Paul's exhortation to the Corinthians, "Test yourselves to see if you are in the faith; examine yourselves."[11]

...if there is no life change, if those disciples haven't moved off their couches to follow Jesus, they're no better off than the demons.

This exhortation for self-examination is not an isolated concept in Scripture. The Bible is rich with many other examples.

> *Examine me, O LORD, and try me; Test my mind and my heart.*
>
> Psalm 26:2

> *Though you probe my heart and examine me at night, though you test me, you will find nothing; I have resolved that my mouth will not sin.*
>
> Psalm 17:3, NIV

> *But, O LORD of hosts, who judges righteously,*
> *Who tries the feelings and the heart.*
>
> Jeremiah 11:20a

> *O let the evil of the wicked come to an end, but establish the righteous; For the righteous God tries the hearts and minds.*
>
> Psalm 7:9

*Let us examine and probe our ways, And let us return to the LORD.*

Lamentations 3:40

*Search me, O God, and know my heart; Try me and know my anxious thoughts.*

Psalm 139:23

## The Measurements of Authentic Discipleship

Understanding what it means to "measure up" as a follower of Jesus will provide us with tremendous confidence. I believe God wants us to be secure as His disciples.[12] Let's take a journey in the next few chapters to see what measuring up is all about.

# Knowing

*The word disciple does not necessarily mean a believer.*
Kenneth Wuest

As a high school freshman I learned very quickly what the statement, "It's not what you know, but who you know," means. At my small Christian high school, life revolved around the unspoken pecking order. If a freshman stepped out of line, the seniors would quickly remind him that he was only slightly above toilet water. That was the norm. The only exception was if you knew the seniors. In this case, as long as you didn't wear your connections with arrogance, you were considered exempt from much of the friendly hazing that took place.

I was lucky to have freshmen friends who had older brothers in the senior class. As a result, we walked the halls as kings. Of course, if a senior came into our presence, we reverted back to scum.

One day during our freshman year we had a new kid transfer into our small school. He was from Florida, and he was different, to say the least. He knew a lot about life and the street compared to us sheltered Midwestern kids. This new guy brought his Florida nickname with him into our school. He told us to call him "Butch," and we did. We didn't fear him, but we did have a distant respect, and we were somewhat in awe of him. After all, he knew a lot more than we did.

*The problem was he didn't really know his place.* He was a freshman after all, and a new freshman at that. He didn't lower his eyes when the seniors walked by. He didn't know about the pecking order. Maybe he didn't care. Regardless, even though Butch knew a lot, he didn't know the people who mattered. As a result, he was picked on.

## Ancient Day Freshmen

In a way, the Pharisees of Jesus' day could have been nicknamed "Butch." Like the kid from high school, they didn't know their place either. I don't think they started out all bad. They had an intense passion for the Law, personal holiness, and following God. The crazy thing was that their knowledge of the Law actually prevented them from getting to know God.

The Pharisees knew the teachings of God and yet failed to see the Christ they prophesied about.

It was as if they relied on what they knew and forgot whom they were supposed to be getting to know. Their religion soon replaced God. As their heads grew bigger, their hearts became colder. Things got so bad that when Jesus showed up on the scene, they didn't even recognize Him. These experts in the Law, the men who knew all sorts of details about the coming Messiah, missed Him even when He was standing right in front of them. The Pharisees knew the teachings of God and yet failed to see the Christ they prophesied about. This disconnection angered Jesus, and He let them know it.

> *You search the Scriptures because you think that in them you have eternal life; it is these that testify about Me; and you are unwilling to come to Me that you may have life.*
>
> John 5:39-40

Jesus recognized their knowledge of the Scriptures. He made it clear to the Pharisees, however, that just because they knew about God, didn't mean that they also knew Him. Jesus was a mirror that exposed the Pharisees for who they really were.

*It is My Father who glorifies Me, of whom you say, "He is our God"; and you have not come to know Him…*
John 8:54b-55a



Let's not blame the Pharisees too much though. In seminary I read many books by many scholars. These men and women were brilliant when it came to the culture, archaeology, and languages surrounding the biblical text. Some wrote commentaries, articles, and volumes about the apostles, prophets, and even Jesus. Yet, many of these geniuses, who knew so much, failed to know Jesus. Some believed that He was just a good teacher. Many believed the Bible was merely another piece of literature.

*Knowledge alone doesn't dictate spirituality.*

Knowledge alone doesn't dictate spirituality. Paul warned that knowledge makes one arrogant.[1] He placed love at a much higher level, stating that it edifies. In a different letter, Paul wrote about a certain group of people who were always learning. Rather than complimenting them, he explained that despite their learning, they never came to a place where they possessed knowledge of the truth.[2] Paul warned other believers against spending their time in debate about endless genealogies, fables, or myths that are often linked to a pursuit of excessive knowledge.[3]

With all these strikes against knowledge and knowing, you would think followers of Jesus should steer clear of it. Quite the contrary. The Bible exhorts us to consider knowing to be a key aspect of *how* we measure up and *if* we measure up as disciples. I believe it is the *first* measurement in the discipleship process. All other measurements flow from our knowing. We can't become, do, or reproduce what we do not first know. Therefore, even though there are cautions with respect to knowing, it is fundamental in shaping us as followers of Jesus.

## The Baby and the Bathwater

Although we must become like children to enter the kingdom of heaven, we dare not remain like children.[4] The author of Hebrews was frustrated with his readers' lack of knowledge.

Regarding their knowledge of spiritual things, figuratively they ought to have been consuming solid food, but instead they were like babies, still dependent upon milk.[5]

It seems as though the recipients of the book of Hebrews, although disciples, lacked knowledge. Even though they "ought to be teachers, [they] have need again for someone to teach [them] the elementary principles of the oracles of God."[6] In the mind of the Holy Spirit, as evidenced through the inspiration of the human author who penned the words in the book of Hebrews, disciples should increase in their knowledge of God and His Word. There should be a progression in our knowing. One outcome of our knowing is that we'll be able to teach others. The recipients of the book of Hebrews were lacking in this area. They didn't measure up.

*One can have every theology degree available, but still miss Christ and end up in hell.*

God takes the knowing process seriously. In the Old Testament He identified lack of knowledge as the main reason His people, the Israelites, were destroyed. He disqualified them from serving as His priests because they did not take knowledge seriously.

> *My people are destroyed for lack of knowledge. Because you have rejected knowledge, I also will reject you from being My priest. Since you have forgotten the law of your God, I also will forget your children.*
>
> Hosea 4:6

Knowing is what sets a disciple of Christ apart from a disciple of Buddha or Mohammed. All disciples know something, but it's what they know, or better, *whom* they know, that distinguishes them from everyone else. As followers of Jesus, our knowing must lead us somewhere. Many arrogant women and men have a tremendous amount of knowledge about spiritual things, even the teachings of Christ. The greatest hypocrites are often the individuals who know the most about the Bible.

Cult leaders typically possess a vast knowledge of the Bible. But knowledge alone does not guarantee discipleship. Even the demons and the demon-possessed had deep knowledge about spiritual things but failed to be authentic disciples.[7]

Our knowing must go beyond head knowledge. There are many verses that teach us about where our knowledge should lead.[8] If it doesn't lead us somewhere, essentially to Christ, then we're in great danger. One can have every theology degree available, but still miss Christ and end up in hell. It is not our knowing that saves us. It's not our knowing alone that determines if we measure up as true disciples. Knowing is a crucial piece of the puzzle, but it's only a piece. There are three other essential pieces that make up our paradigm as well.

> *I am the good shepherd, and I know My own*
> *and My own know Me.*
>
> John 10:14

# Being

*Waste no more time arguing what*
*a good man should be. Be one.*
Marcus Aurelius

As I think back to my childhood, I was a kid of many quirks. I remember having the ability to recall my surroundings exceptionally well. I was great at distinguishing landmarks. I could remember a particular park or a McDonald's restaurant that my family had visited only once. I had a problem though. I couldn't give directions very well. I had a tough time telling my right from my left.

One time my family had out-of-town guests over for an afternoon. They stayed for a long time and the dinner hour was fast approaching. Our guests insisted they drive to the nearest KFC and pick up chicken for everyone. I quickly piped up and volunteered to direct them to KFC.

I felt very important sitting shotgun and having the fate of our dinner rest on my navigational skills. I had the directions for KFC down cold. When the time came for us to make the necessary turn, our guest asked whether he should turn right or left, I froze. I didn't know what to tell him. I knew where we needed to go; I just forgot whether the turn was to our left or to our right. I remember feeling like a loser when he turned the wrong way. I had a stupid directional quirk!

Another quirk of mine involved a homemade superhero cape. I don't remember who made it for me, probably one of my mom's friends. I have several pictures and many memories of wearing that cape. One side of the cape was red for Superman. The other side was blue for Batman. When I wore the Superman side, I had X-ray vision and the power to fly. When I wore the Batman side, I had the power to do...Batman stuff.

My quirk came when I tried distinguishing which side I was wearing. To me it didn't matter what side was showing to the rest of the world. All I cared about was when I turned my neck and looked down. I'd see the color red and think I was Superman when everyone else saw the blue side and called me Batman. I was a confused kid, to say the least.

I remember getting in fights with my cousin Johnny when we played superheroes. In the midst of an intense battle scene, I'd take on the respective personality and powers inherent to the superhero I thought I was. He'd tell me I wasn't that person. I'd turn my neck and look down at the cape to see who was right. I'd defend myself and my personality. He'd try to convince me that I wasn't who I said I was. Johnny was right. I was wrong.

## Who Are You?

I think most people don't know who they are. Like me and my cape, many disciples are looking at other things to find out who they are. Just as my cape had two sides that represented two people with completely different personalities, so many disciples of Jesus are playing a similar game. At times they want to call the shots. They want to follow their own agenda, their own dreams, and their own desires. They want to be in control of their lives. At other times, when it's convenient, they want to follow Jesus and let Him call the shots. As with me and my cape, they're confused. In the battle of life they often try to defend their actions. In reality many of them are not who they say they are. The great equalizer that brings clarity to this phenomenon is the second measurement in our paradigm, *being*. Scripture doesn't allow us to claim that we're disciples in our knowing and not in our being. On the contrary, Scripture states that true disciples are those who are becoming changed in their being.

We are born again to become something great. We are born to have Christ formed inside us.

> *[You have] put on the new self who is being renewed*
> *to a true knowledge according to the image of the One who*
> *created him.*
>
> Colossians 3:10

Allowing Christ to be formed in us requires hard work. We cannot sit around, doing nothing, waiting for God to change us. A disciple is a follower, so we must be followers, especially in our being. It's a divine partnership of sorts. God is working in us to change us, and we must work out the reality of that in our lives.

> *Work out your salvation with fear and trembling;*
> *for it is God who is at work in you, both to will and*
> *to work for His good pleasure.*
>
> Philippians 2:12c-13

Paul is referring to our sanctification. Although sanctification starts with our knowing, it must quickly move into our being, otherwise it remains only theoretical. Eventually it will move into our doing and reproducing as well, but that will be addressed in later chapters.

Just like the measurement of knowing is dangerous if it remains all by itself, so it is with the measurement of being. It too is only a piece of the puzzle.

## Modern Day Monks

Several times throughout church history there has been an intense emphasis upon *being* a disciple of Jesus. This focus was often incarnated in the monastic life. Based on Matthew 4:1-11, some as early as the fifth century said that Jesus was the first monk.[1] In following Christ, from the time of Saint Anthony the Great in A.D. 285, men and women have pursued the monastic life.[2] A monk's entire life was centered upon developing the internal.[3] "The monk renounced the world and flees from human company."[4]

Why did monks choose this way of life? "The monks themselves would reply that they could better serve their fellow human beings by ceaselessly holding them in prayer than by engaging in much busyness and activity."[5] Certainly, an intense focus upon spiritual formation is commendable. Too often in our busy culture, that seems to be the last thing believers focus on. With this in mind, should we all adopt the monastic way of life?

*...the moment we try to repay grace is the moment it ceases to be grace.*

The New Testament seems to speak against the premise that discipleship is simply about being spiritual. James 2:14-18 says that spirituality is dead if it fails to be linked with right doing. Spiritual formation, at the expense of right doing, is spiritual deformation! Separating from the world is not the answer. Authentic discipleship cannot be reduced merely to living in a cell under a vow of silence, reading and studying the Scriptures.

There are always dangers in pursuing discipleship. There are some who try to accomplish spiritual formation in the strength of the flesh. Others try to turn sanctification into a means of repaying God's grace. It's ironic, but the moment we try to repay grace is the moment it ceases to be grace.

Just because there are some dangers doesn't mean we should swing the pendulum the other way. The Bible endorses spiritual disciplines. It requires integrity in our being. God wants us to be holy. After all, we're supposed to be His followers, and He is holy.

> *But like the Holy One who called you, be holy yourselves*
> *also in all your behavior; because it is written,*
> *"You shall be holy, for I am holy."*
>
> 1 Peter 1:15-16

Following Jesus takes effort. But thankfully God meets us in the process. He doesn't leave us on our own.

## Partakers of the Divine

Much of becoming disciples is working out what God is already working in. God doesn't just tell us to be holy. He doesn't set the bar high and walk away, waiting for us to fail. He puts His divine nature within every believer.

*For by these He has granted to us His precious and magnificent promises, so that by them you may become partakers of the divine nature, having escaped the corruption that is in the world by lust.*

2 Peter 1:4

We have two natures this side of heaven. We're battling the flesh, and we'll never be fully like Him until we die and are glorified. That is the culmination of our salvation. In the Western world we often see salvation as the point in time when we choose to accept Jesus. But this is only part of the story.

When we choose to follow Jesus as our Lord and Savior, we're justified. The rest of life, we're in the process of becoming more and more holy. That is sanctification. The day we die or are raptured, we will be glorified. Thus, believers have been saved; they are being saved; and they will be saved. This threefold process is the essence of salvation.

Essentially, this side of heaven, believers should be in a continual state of becoming. That is what salvation is all about. None of us will completely measure up until we are glorified. That should encourage us. But it hardly means that we wait till heaven to start living like Jesus. Doug Pagitt addresses this in *Reimagining Spiritual Formation*. "I used to think it was hypocritical for people to confess Christian belief out loud and then not live up to it. In most cases, however, people are in a state of becoming, not a state of hypocrisy."[6]

Sadly, the Western church often presents salvation exclusively as justification. Receive Jesus and then go on your merry way until you die. Like a State Farm insurance policy, we place the security of our future in the hands of our agent (Jesus) and are happy that He also paid our premium in full. That is a rather depressing view of salvation. Scripture presents salvation much differently. The Bible refers to all three aspects as salvation. It doesn't separate them.

It refers to **justification** as salvation: *In Him, you also, after listening to the message of truth, the gospel of your* salvation—*having also believed, you were sealed in Him with the Holy Spirit of promise.* Ephesians 1:13

It refers to **sanctification** as salvation: *So then, my beloved, just as you have always obeyed, not as in my presence only, but now much more in my absence, work out your* salvation *with fear and trembling; for it is God who is at work in you, both to will and to work for His good pleasure.* Philippians 2:12-13

And it refers to **glorification** as salvation: *Do this, knowing the time, that it is already the hour for you to awaken from sleep; for now* salvation *is nearer to us than when we believed.* Romans 13:11

Each of these passages uses the English word "salvation." Yet each passage refers to a different aspect of salvation. Justification is freedom from the *penalty* of sin. Sanctification is freedom from the *power* of sin. Glorification is freedom from the *presence* of sin. The complete process is salvation. That is part of the reason there is so much confusion regarding salvation and discipleship. People think they received Jesus one time by walking down the aisle, and now they're good to go. In reality, that is only the first step. We don't accept Jesus. We follow Him. God is the one who accepts us because of Jesus. Justification isn't the end of the process; it's only the beginning

People think they received Jesus one time by walking down the aisle, and now they're good to go.

Salvation is like a bride on her wedding day. Scripture refers to all followers of Jesus as His bride. The bride does not wring her hands on the way out of the church and claim, "I am glad I got that taken care of." Instead, the wedding day is only the beginning of the adventure. The bride has tremendous excitement about the couple's new life together.

Salvation is similar. Justification is the first step that begins the relationship. We enter into a sacred covenant with our groom, Jesus Christ. However, salvation is also life together. It is the process of becoming. And thank God, it's eternal life together as well. We cheapen salvation, and I think we even distort it, when we present it merely as a fire insurance policy to escape the flames of hell. (See chart on next page for more insight regarding salvation).

## REGARDING SALVATION

| Component | Quality of Life | Process | Freedom From | Point in Time |
|---|---|---|---|---|
| Justification | Immediate Life | Have Been Saved | Penalty of Sin | Past |
| Sanctification | Abundant Life | Am Being Saved | Power of Sin | Present |
| Glorification | Eternal Life | Will be Saved | Presence of Sin | Future |

The beauty of salvation is transformation. God promises that we will be changed. Who we are, regarding our position in Christ, is drastically changed the moment we are regenerated. We're changed from death to life, from darkness to light. This transformation is not something we feel. Although it happens in an instant, the practical outworking is much slower. Regardless, we're given a new heart.

This transformation is not something we feel. Although it happens in an instant, the practical outworking is much slower.

> *And I will give them one heart, and put a new spirit within them. And I will take the heart of stone out of their flesh and give them a heart of flesh, that they may walk in My statutes and keep My ordinances, and do them. Then they will be My people, and I shall be their God.*
> Ezekiel 11:19-20

Paul tells us, in 2 Corinthians 3:2-3, that "we are letters of Christ." He explains that we are not written upon with ink but rather with "the Spirit of the living God." And quite intimately, it is upon our hearts where the Spirit writes Himself. The blessing is that God makes the commitment to change us. He says He'll finish what He has started within us.[7] It's not that we adopt a mode of striving in order to repay God. Rather, as we rest in Him and His power, we will be changed day by day into His image. Our position is secure. And God puts His word within us.

*But the word is very near you, in your mouth and in your heart, that you may observe it.*

Deuteronomy 30: 14

## The Process

We begin the process of discipleship through our knowing. We hear the call of Jesus. He comes to us saying, "Follow Me." We have a choice. Will we follow Him, or will we continue the way we've always lived? Christ gives us an option. He appeals to our freedom of choice. We cognitively process His call. We review His statement in our heads. What gives Him the authority? What is so appealing about His offer? Why are our spirits quickened with those two simple words? We think. We ponder. Some of us choose to stay. Some of us choose to follow.

Quickly we find out that following Jesus is not merely about our heads. We begin and continue the journey with our heads, but we must allow our hearts to be engaged as well. We allow Jesus to saturate our knowing and we also give Him permission to saturate our being. We follow Him with our being. We allow head knowledge to become heart knowledge. We soon embody Christ. He takes up residence within us, and we give Him room to form Himself within us.

The natural outflow of Jesus taking up residence in our knowing and being is for Jesus to seep into our doing. Forget the striving. Forget the flesh. We're not mercenaries warring against our sinful natures. We're not God's special agents in a militia that battles the flesh. Rather, we're His temple. We're jars of clay that host the Divine. There's nothing in us that deserves this privilege. We're but dust. Yet this is salvation. This is the beauty. Because we're in Christ, what we do in this life should be what Jesus would do. This leads us to the next measurement in our paradigm.

*Let your heart therefore be wholly devoted*
*to the LORD our God,*
*to walk in His statutes and to keep*
*His commandments, as at this day.*

1 Kings 8:61

# Doing

*Example is the most powerful rhetoric.*
Thomas Brooks

I'll be honest. I'm made of clay just like everyone else. I don't think this comes as a surprise. I'll demonstrate this with a personal example of how frustrated I can be with a certain type of person. There is probably nothing that frustrates me more than someone who talks big but has no action. God occasionally puts people like that into my life. Maybe it's to teach me patience. Maybe it's to reveal my own sin and pride. In any case, it still bugs me big time when I encounter such a person.

You can find this type of person in all walks of life. He or she can be a retiree, a student, or a business executive. Regardless, this type of person has certain innate characteristics. If she's an athlete, she's usually the one sitting on the bench injured. She'll liberally expound on how so and so on the field should have done this or that differently. She will go on and on about her past athletic achievements. When you ask her why she's on the bench, she'll go into detail about her injury and why she can't practice with the rest of the team.

This type of person could be a pastor. He'll talk for hours about how he has no time for himself because his congregation needs him so badly. He'll tell you story after story about all the sacrifices he has made to advance the cause of Christ. He'll let you know that his sermon preparation has suffered because Sunday snuck up on him without warning. He was so busy suffering for Jesus, he couldn't study God's Word. Instead of preaching the Bible, his sermon will simply be his most recent soapbox philosophies.

I'll give you one more example just to be sure you get the picture. This person is often an aspiring musician. Such a person drops names about all the big stars she knows in the recording industry. She explains how she plans to sell everything in order to go to Nashville and make it big. She has the look, the clothes, and the tattoos to play the part. Each time you see her, the story gets grander and grander, and she gives you one more excuse why she hasn't made it yet.

What is it about such a person that annoys me? I think what bugs me so much is that I don't like people who talk big, but never deliver. I feel people should let their actions do their talking. As the athletic adages go, "Put up or shut up." "Walk the walk; don't just talk the talk."

## If We All Were Wrestlers

I wish I could take these big talker types to a wrestling tournament. I wrestled all through high school. In my freshman and sophomore years I was guilty at times of being one of those big talker types. I'd walk off the mat after losing my match and begin to talk. I'd tell others why the referee made me lose. I'd talk about how he missed the call or scored a takedown when he shouldn't have.

Wrestling can be a subjective sport. It's not like basketball, where you either make the basket or you don't. It's not like baseball, where you either hit the ball over the fence or you don't. Wrestling is fast paced and often a referee will make a quick call that could go either way. A big talker wrestler goes on and on, making excuses why he didn't win. He blames it on other factors, whether it's because of his opponent, the lighting, the scorekeeper, or because his singlet got bunched up.

I finally got sick of hearing my excuses. I decided my junior and senior year I'd stop being one of those big talkers. I'd stop blaming others about why I wasn't doing my best.

That totally changed the way I wrestled. Instead of making excuses, I took full responsibility for how I wrestled, whether it was good or bad.

I think wrestling coaches must have gotten sick of hearing excuses from their wrestlers. The reason I'm betting on this is because of the wrestling T-shirts I've seen. I'm always inspired when I read T-shirts at wrestling tournaments. If you ever come across one of those "big talker types" please spare us all and buy them a wrestling T-shirt.

Some of the livelier wrestling T-shirts say things like *Talk is cheap* or *Champions don't talk, they perform.* Although slightly offensive, there is the *Bustin' mine to kick yours* wrestling T-shirt. There is the unkind *No regret, no remorse, no mercy* shirt. And my all-time favorite is the long-winded shirt that defines a wrestler as, *One who trains like a maniac to force his opponent's body into the shape of a pretzel and gently pin him into a soft mat where his mommy can tuck him in.*

These T-shirts all expose the big talker types. They confront them in the area where they are lacking—action! I think Gandhi would have liked wrestling T-shirts. He didn't like big talkers either. I think Gandhi must have met some big talker Christians. Gandhi once said that if it weren't for Christians, he'd be one. Sadly, many big talker Christians have been guilty of telling the world to do as they say and not as they do.

*Gandhi once said that if it weren't for Christians, he'd be one.*

## Brother From Another Mother

In the mind and ministry of Jesus, *doing* was tremendously important. Jesus referred to those who *did* the Word of God as those who were closer than His physical family.[1] He referred to them as His true brothers and sisters, even His friends.[2] He promised that such people would be happy and blessed.[3]

The Christian life is meant to be lived out. "The primary purpose of education in Bible times was to train the whole person for lifelong, obedient service in the knowledge of God."[4] Christianity doesn't exist within theoretical or philosophical debates. "In Hebrew thought to 'know' something was to experience it rather than merely intellectualize it."[5] True Christianity isn't the stuff of seminary classrooms or church Bible studies. Although that may be part of the knowing process, our knowing must be incarnated into everyday life. Even the sacrament of the Bread and the Cup is a participatory event. Jesus said, "This is My body, which is for you; *do* this in remembrance of Me" (emphasis added).[6] Baptism is an action as well. It's a demonstration. It's an outward sign of an inward change.

Jesus never intended Christianity to be a spectator sport. Some might argue that Jesus was angry at a faith devoid of doing. He confronted this inconsistency by asking such people, "Why do you call Me, 'Lord, Lord,' and do not do what I say?"[7] It's not that Jesus was trying to be rude or unkind. It's just that He knew that people who were disciples only in their knowing and being were not really disciples at all.

> *Everyone who comes to Me and hears My words and acts on them, I will show you whom he is like: he is like a man building a house, who dug deep and laid a foundation upon the rock; and when a flood occurred, the torrent burst against that house and could not shake it, because it had been well built. But the one who has heard, and has not acted accordingly, is like a man who built a house upon the ground without any foundation; and the torrent burst against it and immediately it collapsed, and the ruin of that house was great.*
>
> Luke 6:47-49

Such people are destined for destruction. The apostle John writes about an entire church devoid of doing. Its deeds were neither hot nor cold. It was simply going through the motions. The church of Laodicea, found in the book of Revelation, did not receive a warm greeting. Christ said to that church, "I know your deeds, that you are neither cold nor hot; I wish that you were cold or hot. So because you are lukewarm, and neither hot nor cold, I will spit you out of My mouth."[8]

If Gandhi went to church, he wouldn't have attended the one in Laodicea. That church was filled with big talkers. They should have purchased some wrestling T-shirts that said, *Talk is cheap.* That might have reminded them about their need for action.

Scripture says our actions actually bring credibility to our message. God's plan is that we silence the ignorance of foolish people by our right doing. It's not our picketing or boycotting that convinces people we're His disciples. Rather, it's our love.[9] If we lack love, then the Bible says that we don't know God, for God is love.[10]

It's not our picketing or boycotting that convinces people we're His disciples. Rather, it's our love.

People can say they have love; they can say they know what love is. But the Bible distinguishes between those who know and those who do. It separates the hearers from the doers.

> *For it is not the hearers of the Law who are just before God, but the doers of the Law will be justified.*
> Romans 2:13

It's not our doing that saves us. If that were true, Christianity would not be different from any other religion. But Christianity is much different. Our doing *proves* that we're saved. It is not our doing that makes us His disciples. Rather it's our doing that *proves* we're His disciples.

Don't forget the progression of our paradigm. It starts with knowing. We first come to know God's Word. The Bible says, "Faith comes by hearing, and hearing by the Word of God."[11] It can't stop there though. Our knowing must become part of our being. It should become part of who we are. If we're authentic disciples, it *must* become part of who we are. When it does, we become partakers of the divine nature.[12] The Scriptures say "partakers." We're not completely transformed, this side of heaven. That happens during the final aspect of our salvation, at glorification. But because we're partakers, our doing is a supernatural by-product and we no longer have to strive to do good works. As we walk in the Spirit, we no longer carry out the desire of our flesh.[13]

Neither our salvation nor our status as disciples is maintained by what we do. If this were so, none of us would measure up. Still, as our knowing and being become patterned after Christ, there should be a change in our behavior. If we have the Spirit living inside us, as we yield to Him we should have a growing desire to act like Him.

Our doing proves that we're His disciples. Our confidence and our strength flow from Christ. Lest we forget, all our doing is through Christ who gives us strength.[14] We're crucified with Christ.[15] We now have the power to say no to sin. We're no longer slaves to our doing.[16] Instead, our doing should be slaves to Christ.[17]

A faith without works is no faith at all. Scripture says it is dead.[18] When we have a faith devoid of doing, in reality we're spiritually dead. Faith and works are two sides of the same coin. Similarly, for the true disciple, knowing and doing are two sides of the same coin. The reason most of us separate the two is because of our Western worldview. The first-century Jew didn't have this problem. In the Hebrew mind the relationship between faith and works made perfect sense. In *The Ascent of a Leader*, the authors describe the difference between the Greek and Hebrew mind-set.

> In Hebrew philosophy, a belief was not a belief until it was acted on. And all beliefs affected community, because the actions they spawned affected every area of life. In Greek philosophy, belief could be separated from action. Thought and action suffered a painful divorce into upper and lower stories of existence. Greek thinking led to dualism, a separation between the material and spiritual aspects of life. The material world—the realm of the senses and action—declined in value. The spiritual world—the realm of the mind and emotions—represented a higher plane of existence. The work of earning daily bread played second fiddle to the pursuit of philosophy. Greek thought infiltrated the early Church

> and gave birth to a separate class of priests, clerics, and a host of monastic orders. This thinking still pervades modern society and the Church in a variety of ways. The Hebrew philosophy seems comparatively simple. No dualism. No separation. If you love someone, you will meet her need. If you meet someone's need, you love her. Hebrews did not separate the heart from the mind, or belief from action. They were one in the same. What you believed affected all you did, from cooking a meal to building a city. What you did reflected what you believed. Therefore, work became an act of worship, and no vocation was viewed as more sacred or higher than another.[19]

One of my friends, an avid world traveler, helped me understand the difference between the Greek and Hebrew mind through the common everyday situation of convincing one's neighbor it is going to rain. Assume such a conversation happens at the local café. In the Greek mind-set, the individual informing her neighbor would refer to the common weather patterns this time of year, the pressure systems, and the weather instruments that all predict the coming rainstorm. She would talk to her neighbor using logic, scientific rules, and an appeal to reason. From these proofs she would convince her neighbor it is going to rain. She would arrive at this conclusion from the basis of their discussion.

*The Hebrew mind-set is much different. In reality it is much simpler.*

The Hebrew mind-set is much different. In reality it is much simpler. A person would convince her neighbor it is going to rain by simply carrying an umbrella to the café. It is not an appeal to logic that convinces the Hebrew mind. Rather, it is the simple action that demonstrates belief.

So it is with authentic disciples. Of course, such people know the Word of God. It has to start there. But it is our doing, flowing from our being, which demonstrates our authenticity as His disciples. "To 'know' God is to walk faithfully in his ways and to live out the terms of his covenant."[20] We can forget lecturing others about how we walked the aisle to receive Jesus 15 years ago. It's our action that does all the talking.

> *But someone may well say, "You have faith, and I have works; show me your faith without the works, and I will show you my faith by my works." You believe that God is one. You do well; the demons also believe, and shudder. But are you willing to recognize, you foolish fellow, that faith without works is useless?*
>
> James 2:18-20

## Beyond the Steeple

That doesn't mean we always have to be praying, reading our Bibles, or singing in order to be disciples. Right doing must include the mundane things of life as well. All of life can and should be the bread and butter of what constitutes authentic discipleship. If not, then our spirituality becomes confined to a church building. That type of Christianity is dangerous indeed.

Francis Schaeffer wrote, "A platonic concept of spirituality which does not include all of life is not true biblical spirituality. True spirituality touches all of life...not just 'religious' things."[21] Abraham Kuyper added to this concept by stating, "There is not an inch in the entire domain of our human life of which Christ, who is sovereign of all, does not proclaim, 'Mine!'"[22]

"True spirituality touches all of life... not just 'religious' things."

These scholars understood that Christ must intersect all of what we do in life. Spirituality and right doing must impact the movies we watch, the sports we play, and the jobs we work. Right doing even touches what we eat and how we eat. All of life, the big things and the small things, relate to discipleship.

*Whether, then, you eat or drink or whatever you do, do all to the glory of God.*

1 Corinthians 10:31

## Time to Procreate

This leads to our fourth and final measurement. Remember, our paradigm reveals how discipleship is measured. If we're authentic disciples, then we must be followers of Jesus in our knowing, being, doing, *and* reproducing. No one lives out his or her discipleship in a vacuum. God's original plan in Eden was that every person would have the capability to reproduce other people, so it is also His plan in the church that every disciple have the capability to reproduce other disciples.

*And God said to them, "Be fruitful and multiply, and fill the earth..."*

Genesis 1:28a

*And Jesus... spoke to them, saying, "Go therefore and make disciples of all the nations..."*

Matthew 28:18a, 19a

# Reproducing

*What is spent is gone. What I kept is lost.*
*But what I gave will be mine forever.*
Epitaph on a tombstone

In Genesis 1 there is a curious phrase repeated several times in the creation story (see vv. 11, 12, 21, 24, 25). Whether God was making trees or cattle, He commanded them to make more "after their own kind." There is a profound concept within these four words. God's original intent was that every living thing reproduce. It is natural for living things to reproduce after their own kind. In other words, cats reproduce cats, giraffes reproduce giraffes, orange trees reproduce orange trees, and believers reproduce believers.

This isn't a new phenomenon. Most people know DNA reproduces like DNA. If one has the DNA of an elephant, then an elephant will be reproduced. If one has the DNA of a snake, then a snake will be reproduced. If one is a follower of Jesus in her knowing, being, and doing, then she should also reproduce others who are followers of Jesus in their knowing, being, and doing.

In the book of Genesis God emphasized being fruitful and multiplying. Ironically, when God created plants, animals, and people in Eden, He created them in a mature state, with the ability to reproduce. The plants were created "with the seed in them."[1]

God didn't create seeds or saplings. He created plant life ready to reproduce.

Adam and Eve weren't created as babies or kids who hadn't reached puberty. They were created as a mature man and woman with the capability to reproduce and were commanded to do so. Somehow, it's a spiritual thing to reproduce. It's part of our duty as stewards. The context of marriage sanctifies the act of physical procreation. Reproduction is an important role of all living things, whether plants, animals, or people.

I think every living person automatically reproduces disciples. Remember, a disciple is a follower. All humans influence others to follow them. Whether it's subtle or straightforward, conscious or unconscious, intentional or accidental, each one of us is affecting others simply because we're alive. Some of us are more strategic than others, but we are all shaping other followers.

There is an old anti-drug commercial that reflects this phenomenon. An upset father finds some drugs in his son's room. Frantically, he moves through the house looking for his son. When he finds him, he's violently upset and demands, "Where did you learn how to do this?" There is a long pause. In a chilling response his son says, "From you, Dad. I learned it from you." As the camera pans out, the viewer is struck by the reality that we're all reproducing ourselves in others, our good habits as well as our bad ones.

## The Good, the Bad, and the Ugly

The Bible provides many examples of people who reproduced others after their own kind. The Old Testament highlights king after king who walked in the way of his father. When the father was good, this behavior was often reproduced in his son. Unfortunately, when the father was evil, evil behavior was reproduced in his son. The truth is that our behavior causes some to stumble and others to succeed.

> *But as for you, you have turned aside from the way; you have caused many to stumble by the instruction; you have corrupted the covenant of Levi," says the* Lord *of hosts.*
>
> Malachi 2:8

The question is not *whether* we're making disciples. The real question is *what type* of disciples are we making? Reproducing is not the fourth measurement by accident. If we're followers of Christ in our knowing, being, and doing, then most likely we will reproduce other disciples who are followers of Christ also. If we fail to be authentic disciples of Christ, then most likely we'll reproduce followers who also fail to be authentic disciples of Christ.

*The question is not whether we're making disciples. The real question is what type of disciples are we making?*

God has always been passionate about reproducing a godly remnant. He built structures within the Jewish framework so mothers and fathers could reproduce children who feared the Lord. Civil laws, ceremonial observances, and religious rituals were often intentionally geared in such a way to promote instruction, discussion, and interaction between parent and child. This was done to reinforce the potential for reproducing godly disciples.

> *Fix these words of mine in your hearts and minds; tie them as symbols on your hands and bind them on your foreheads.*
>
> *Teach them to your children, talking about them when you sit at home and when you walk along the road, when you lie down and when you get up.*
>
> *Write them on the doorframes of your houses and on your gates, so that your days and the days of your children may be many in the land that the LORD swore to give your forefathers, as many as the days that the heavens are above the earth.*
>
> *If you carefully observe all these commands I am giving you to follow – to love the LORD your God, to walk in all his ways and to hold fast to him…*
>
> Deuteronomy 11:18-22 (NIV)

## Nothing to Fear

People are always watching us, and because of this, we always have the potential of making disciples. That can be a scary thought. If we stop to consider the implications of such a concept, it can cause us to feel pressured, like we're under the gun or under the microscope. In a way, each one of us is the main character in the story of our lives. Whether for good or bad, the world reads us and observes our lives. Paul recognized this, and instead of resisting it, he seemed to embrace it.

> *But we proved to be gentle among you, as a nursing mother tenderly cares for her own children. Having so fond an affection for you, we were well-pleased to impart to you not only the gospel of God but also our own lives, because you had become very dear to us. For you recall, brethren, our labor and hardship, how working night and day so as not to be a burden to any of you, we proclaimed to you the gospel of God.You are witnesses, and so is God, how devoutly and uprightly and blamelessly we behaved toward you believers; just as you know how we were exhorting and encouraging and imploring each one of you as a father would his own children.*
>
> 1 Thessalonians 2:7-11

> *For you yourselves know how you ought to follow our example, because we did not act in an undisciplined manner among you, nor did we eat anyone's bread without paying for it, but with labor and hardship we kept working night and day so that we would not be a burden to any of you; not because we do not have the right to this, but in order to offer ourselves as a model for you, that you might follow our example.*
>
> 2 Thessalonians 3:7-9

Earlier in my life, I felt the pressure of being watched. I knew those around me, saved or unsaved, were examining my life. As a result, I tried to perform. I played the main character in my carefully constructed story. It wasn't natural and I concealed all the bad things: the anger, the frustration, and the pain. I presented a squeaky clean imitation of what I thought Christlikeness should be. Those were sad and empty years. I put myself on a pedestal, and of course, I couldn't measure up.

Our paradigm is not a pedestal we stand on or a goal we work up to. If it were, then it would be no different from any other idol that captures the hearts of God's people. Rather, it acts as a mirror. It reflects how we're doing in terms of holistic, authentic discipleship. It reveals areas where Christ is not reigning. Once these areas are exposed, we dare not try to cover them up. Neither should we muster up performance to bridge the gaps. Instead, we must be honest. We need to let the world know we don't have it all together. What do we have to fear? If we are truly accepted in the Beloved, if there is really no fear in love, if there is truly no condemnation in Christ, then we should be the most open, honest, and transparent people in the world.[2]

*...if there is truly no condemnation in Christ, then we should be the most open, honest, and transparent people in the world.*

Being a disciple doesn't mean being perfect. It just means we know the One who is. If we could get a handle on this, our lives would be changed. We would be less focused on a religious performance for the world and more intent on an authentic following of Jesus. Once the pressure to perform is gone, the natural by-product is that we are able to reflect Jesus in our knowing, being, and doing. Ironically, this is usually the time when we're most effective at reproducing Christ in others. It's at that moment we're able to see lost people not as projects that need converting, but rather as pilgrims that need Jesus, just like us.

> *Tell it to your children, and let your children tell it to their children, and their children to the next generation.*
>
> Joel 1:3 (NIV)

# The Measurement Paradigm

*A master in the art of living draws no sharp distinction between his work and his play; his labor and his leisure; his mind and his body; his education and his recreation. He hardly knows which is which. He simply pursues his vision of excellence through whatever he is doing, and leaves others to determine whether he is working or playing. To himself, he always appears to be doing both.*

Francois Auguste René Chateaubriand

Turn back to page 034 and look again at the measurement paradigm. Notice how each specific measurement is inherently tied to every other measurement. Also, notice that for a stool to support weight, it must have four legs. Three legs will hold some weight, but quite certainly, it's not as stable as four. In order for disciples to be stable, they too must measure up in all four areas. They must be followers of Jesus in their knowing, being, doing, and reproducing. If people measure up only in one area, then they often lean toward an extreme and fail to be true disciples.

| Exclusive Measurement | Tendency of Extreme |
|---|---|
| Knowing | A Pharisee |
| Being | A Monk |
| Doing | A Faith-Based Charity |
| Reproducing | A Baby Machine |

I hope that after reading the previous few chapters, you have come to the conclusion that to be a follower of Jesus in just a couple areas doesn't equate to being an authentic disciple. Biblically, it is clear that many false disciples come having met only one or two measurements. Thus they never attain the status of a true disciple.

Judas was a disciple in his knowing and doing but failed to follow Jesus with his being. As a result, he was never considered an authentic disciple.[1] There is reason to believe that Alexander was a disciple in his being but failed to follow Jesus with his knowing and doing, as evidenced by his blaspheming and evil deeds.[2] In the first century there were many preachers who were followers of Jesus in their knowing and reproducing but were considerably lacking in the area of being. Sadly, during Jesus' ministry many people presented themselves as followers only in their knowing. However, when it came time to be doers, they were excluded from the list of true disciples.[3]

Our purpose here is not to point a finger and determine who's in and who's out. Neither is it a mandate that we all must measure up perfectly in every area. Of course we're all wired differently. Some of us will do better in one measurement than another. In all this, we must keep things in perspective.

Although all disciples continue to develop in Christ, we shouldn't be habitually deficient in any one area of measurement. Today, there are many who follow Jesus with their being, doing, and reproducing who lack a true knowledge of Jesus. They believe Jesus was merely a good teacher. As a result, they too fail to be true disciples. People can't follow Jesus with their heart (being), and hands (doing), but not their heads (knowing). God requires holistic devotion.[4]

Remember, our paradigm can be thought of as a mirror. It will reveal areas where we fail to measure up. The Bible exhorts us to test ourselves to see whether we're in the faith.[5] God didn't give us this command and leave us to guess what He meant by it. Rather, the Scriptures present a complete picture of what it means to be a true follower of Jesus.

## Not Measuring Up

There are times in my life when I see gaps in certain areas. The Holy Spirit convicts me that I'm not measuring up. Sometimes I let the world's philosophies, rather than the mind of Christ, begin to shape my thinking. When this happens, I don't begin to doubt that I'm a true disciple. Rather, it actually gives me more confidence that I *am* a true disciple because I sense conviction.

Let me explain with what might be a weird illustration. If someone is dead physically, he feels nothing. He has no sense of pain or hunger; neither does he feel hot or cold. Likewise, if someone is dead spiritually, he doesn't feel anything either. So, when I sense the Holy Spirit exposing gaps in my knowing, being, doing, or reproducing, it reassures me that I'm alive spiritually. Of course I have a choice when conviction comes. I can blow things off and convince myself that I'm doing great. Or, I can agree with the Spirit about the areas in my life that are not measuring up. It is not my status as a disciple that is being called into question. Rather, it's that if I want to continue following Jesus, then I must do my part and truly follow Him.

In the New Testament we read of Apollos, an eloquent teacher, and a man mighty in the Scriptures. He was a true disciple. He was teaching about Jesus (this is evidence that he was reproducing), yet he was unaware that his knowing needed to increase. He was ignorant about certain truths. Apollos didn't lose his status as a disciple because he failed to have a complete doctrine. Quite the contrary. After he realized that his knowing didn't measure up, the manner in which he responded gave credibility to his authenticity as a disciple.

> *Now a certain Jew named Apollos, an Alexandrian by birth, an eloquent man, came to Ephesus; and he was mighty in the Scriptures. This man had been instructed in the way of the Lord; and being fervent in spirit, he was speaking and teaching accurately the things concerning Jesus, being acquainted only with the baptism of John; and he began to speak out boldly in the synagogue. But when Priscilla and Aquila heard him, they took him aside and explained to him the way of God more accurately. And when he wanted to go*

> *across to Achaia, the brethren encouraged him and wrote to the disciples to welcome him; and when he had arrived, he greatly helped those who had believed through grace, for he powerfully refuted the Jews in public, demonstrating by the Scriptures that Jesus was the Christ.*
>
> Acts 18:24-28

Apollos responded beautifully. He could have been arrogant or stubborn when exposed as not measuring up in a certain area. Instead, he invited others to help increase his knowing. He then adjusted his message and preached more accurately. God blessed him with a tremendous ministry.[6]

Paul was another disciple who lacked in certain areas. Prior to his conversion, Paul's knowing and being didn't measure up. Unlike Apollos though, Paul wasn't even an authentic disciple. He was doing many righteous things. His list of credentials would put many people to shame. He was "circumcised the eighth day, of the nation of Israel, of the tribe of Benjamin, a Hebrew of Hebrews; as to the Law, a Pharisee; as to zeal, a persecutor of the church; as to the righteousness which is in the Law, found blameless."[7] Yet in all this, Paul was not pursuing Jesus. Strangely though, Jesus was pursuing Paul.

Jesus surprised Paul on his way to Damascus.[8] He vividly exposed how Paul didn't measure up. Though Paul thought he was doing great things for God, he didn't even recognize God's voice. Paul asked Him, "Who are You, Lord?" He had a choice. Would he continue on his way, or would he follow Jesus? All believers are beneficiaries of what he chose. This false follower chose to accept the call and become a true follower of Jesus.

## Connect the Unconnected

The beauty of our paradigm lies in the integration of all four measurements. That is what biblical discipleship is all about. Sadly, it isn't what secular discipleship is all about. Greek philosophy is convinced that one can separate knowing from being and doing. This is in sharp contrast to Hebrew philosophy.

When we allow a disconnect to occur among knowing, being, doing, and reproducing, we open the door for tremendous paradox. Take for example the statement, "Do as I say, not as I do." For the Greek philosopher, this concept is perfectly acceptable. It illustrates the dualism between thought and action, knowing and doing.

For the Hebrew philosopher, that statement is illogical and makes no sense at all. One can't say one thing and do another, especially in an authoritarian role. A teacher who professes one thing and incarnates another is a fraud, a fake, or an impostor.

> The beauty of our paradigm lies in the integration of all four measurements.

Thankfully, there is another statement that cuts through the Greek philosophy of dualism. "Your actions speak so loud I can't hear what you say." It is evident that actions speak louder than words. As the old adage goes, "People don't care how much you know until they know how much you care." Society is crying out for models and mentors whose knowing, being, doing, and reproducing harmonize with each other.

Ironically, regarding the desperate need for a holistic, interconnected view of discipleship, the early church probably had a better concept than today's church. Many leaders today have "the false idea that discipleship involves a narrow teaching of ministry skills and accumulation of Bible knowledge."[9] But in the early church, discipleship was measured in terms of its holistic impact on one's life:

> In the Christian communities of the first three centuries, the period prior to one's baptism was often referred to as catechesis, and was a time devoted to instruction about the doctrine and practice of the Church. Catechesis however was more than simply teaching as we think of it; it also incorporated hands-on training in serving the needs of the Christian community. The community of believers played an essential role in training potential members, guiding them toward repentance, and modeling obedience to the way of Christ for them.[10]

This type of training (catechesis) was holistic in nature. Although it included doctrine (knowing), it also included mentoring and ministry. Spiritual formation naturally occurred because of interaction with mature believers. Although individuals played a role in training other individuals, it was the community, more specifically the church, that assumed this responsibility.

Discipleship wasn't a quick process merely involving intellectual assent to a particular set of doctrines. Rather, it was a lengthy, dynamic approach that addressed how followers of Christ allowed Jesus to penetrate their knowing, being, and doing. Discipleship is the "entire manner in which the Gospel becomes a reality in a man's life."[11] Significantly, this educational and evaluative process was done within the context of relationships, which in turn provided a reproductive effect.

## One Without the Other

Regarding authentic discipleship, it is impossible for one to measure up in only a couple areas. People can't follow Jesus with their knowing at the expense of their doing. They must be in concert together. Jesus put right doing on the same level as right knowing. He said, "Not everyone who says to Me, 'Lord, Lord,' will enter the kingdom of heaven, but he who does the will of My Father who is in heaven will enter."[12]

Paul, the apostle who penned much of the New Testament, wrote large portions of his letters to explain the need for right doing. Under the Spirit's inspiration, he told us to do many good things, all of which are part of the call of a Christian. Interestingly, he condemned charitable "right doing," if done at the expense of right being. "And if I give all my possessions to feed the poor, and if I deliver my body to be burned, but do not have love, it profits me nothing."[13] Right being and right doing must go hand in hand.

Right being and right doing must go hand in hand.

Jesus provided a scenario involving right doing at the expense of right knowing. He warned that some would come with the right outward actions. He predicted that false prophets would come like wolves in sheep's clothing.[14] He said they would do great things, even cast out demons and perform miracles. Yet, Jesus will say to them, "I never knew you, depart from me."[15]

None of the four measurements stands independently from any of the other measurements. They are integrated because we must be integrated. Although we try, we can't truly separate who we are from what we do. "The Hasidim have long taught—and rightly so—that a person worships and serves God not simply from the depths of his spirit or soul but with his body and mind as well."[16] We can't truly separate what we know from what we do. If we fail to do something, it is because we haven't truly made it a part of who we are.

God told the Israelites, "Their deeds will not allow them to return to their God."[17] Regardless of how much they wanted to know God, their deficiency in one measurement affected the other areas of measurement.

Solomon was guilty of the same fate. He let down his guard in one area and soon stopped following God. Solomon didn't fail to follow God in his knowing, doing, or reproducing. He never forgot the Law of God. Neither did he stop doing things for God. He didn't even stop reproducing other followers of God. After all Solomon led the nation of Israel into its greatest time of peace and worship of the one true God. Solomon's failure was that he didn't measure up in his being. He slowly let his heart change. As a result, he lost it all.

> *For when Solomon was old, his wives turned his heart away after other gods; and his heart was not wholly devoted to the LORD his God, as the heart of David his father had been.*
>
> 1 Kings 11:4

Scripture reveals people who fail to measure up in all areas. Such people are cast in an unfavorable light.[18] None of us completely measures up in all areas at all times. It is important to note, however, that there is a big difference between an authentic disciple who is trying to improve in an area, and a person who is arrogantly deficient in an area. We can confess God with our mouths and deny Him with our deeds. Likewise, we can prove our knowledge of God by the way we act. The key is holistically following Jesus. That is what discipleship is all about: the head, the heart, and the hands.

In his book, *In Search of the Great Commission*, William L. Banks describes this concept of holistic discipleship:

> To make one a disciple certainly includes the use of the mind, as well as the heart and will. Unless there is a heart change, a change of life-style, a true conversion through faith in the shed blood of Jesus Christ, one cannot become a true disciple. Men may give intellectual assent, and verbal profession, yet not believe in their hearts.[19]

## Four by Four

Each measurement in our paradigm can be found entrenched in the passages below.

> *For Ezra had set his heart to study the law of the LORD, and to practice it, and to teach His statutes and ordinances in Israel.*
>
> Ezra 7:10

> *True instruction was in his mouth and unrighteousness was not found on his lips; he walked with Me in peace and uprightness, and he turned many back from iniquity. For the lips of a priest should preserve knowledge, and men should seek instruction from his mouth; for he is the messenger of the LORD of hosts.*
>
> Malachi 2:6-7

> *Let no one look down on your youthfulness, but rather in speech, conduct, love, faith and purity, show yourself an example of those who believe. Until I come, give attention to the public reading of Scripture, to exhortation and teaching.*
>
> 1 Timothy 4:12-13

These verses clearly express the reality that there is no way to fake authentic discipleship. True disciples are those who follow God in their knowing, being, doing, and reproducing. It's that simple. If we're followers of Jesus in only a couple areas, then we're as unbalanced as a two-legged stool. Not only that, we're also imposters. But as we allow Jesus to integrate and incarnate our lives holistically, we will find that quite naturally we measure up.

> The aim of the Jewish teacher was not so much to develop certain intellectual or practical faculties in his disciple but rather to summon his learner to submit to the authority of the divine message of the Scripture upon which he was commenting… here the Jew's whole personality is involved.
>
> Marvin Wilson

# Part 3

# WHAT ARE THE COMPONENTS OF DISCIPLESHIP?

# The Components

*If you don't like change, you're going to like irrelevance even less.*

General Eric Shinseki, Chief of Staff, U.S. Army.

Early in my marriage, I installed siding on houses to put food on the table. My boss was a kind, generous, and patient man. He did have quirks, though, that often centered on pithy little statements I had never heard before. I don't remember all of them, but one particularly stands out to me. I suppose it's because of the strange mental picture it creates.

In the midst of siding a house, at the weirdest times, my boss would say, "There's more than one way to skin a cat." It's obvious what he was getting at. He was stating that there are a number of methods that will produce the same outcome.

It's no different in discipleship. Alice Fryling, in *Disciplemakers' Handbook*, explains, "Disciplemaking is individualized because no two people learn, change, or grow in exactly the same way. Effective disciplemaking is suited to that uniqueness. It does not come with a prefabricated formula."[1]

There are many different methods for making disciples. Some disciple at coffee shops, others while working out at the gym. A dear friend of mine disciples men while fishing. In discipling others, some prefer a program or workbook and an organized study time. Methods vary, but components don't.

Although there might not be one universal methodology of discipleship, I believe the Bible presents four universal components that represent authentic discipleship and dovetail beautifully with the four measurements already explained. They feed off one another. Our measurement paradigm answers the question, "Are we really disciples?" Our component paradigm answers the question, "What are the elements that make up authentic discipleship?"

We are not addressing how to make disciples. Our two paradigms might provide some insight into answering that question, but that is for another time and place. If one can grasp the measurements and components of authentic discipleship, making disciples will be much easier.

Here is an example that might provide additional clarity. If one can understand how happiness is measured and the components that make up happiness, it's a relatively easy process actually to have happiness. The leap is not that great.

So it is with discipleship. The initial step is to understand the measurements and components that make up discipleship. We've already explored the measurements in detail and now we will explore the components.

The four components of discipleship are theology, spiritual formation, ministry, and coaching. Theology is related to the measurement of knowing. Spiritual formation is related to the measurement of being. Ministry is related to the measurement of doing, and coaching is related to the measurement of reproducing.

As you took a long, hard look at the measurements of discipleship, perhaps you saw areas where you don't fully measure up. That might be considered the bad news. The good news is that God wants you to be a balanced disciple. The four components are vehicles to help achieve that balance. The paradigm on the next page depicts these four components and how they fit together. The remaining chapters unpack the four components in detail.

# The Components of Authentic Discipleship

# Theology

*We live in the age of the overworked and the under educated, the age in which people are so industrious that they become absolutely stupid.*
Oscar Wilde

I have a confession. I used to be an anti-intellectual. I hated reading, studying, and school in general. I thank God that His grace rescued me from such a pitiful state. It's not that I hated thinking; I just didn't do much of it and I was never really taught how.

Think about it. We're taught how to read and write. We're taught how to spell and add. Yet no one really teaches us how to think.

In school I was never one of those kids invited into any of the *smart* classes. I took *general* math, *general* science, and *general* English. *General* was my middle name, that is until I got an invitation from Mr. Moore.

You have to know something about Mr. Moore. He was one of those teachers that the 4.0 kids intentionally avoided. Parents wrote the school administration and requested that their kids be pulled from his class because his teaching antics would often hurt their G.P.A.

I was pretty excited to get an invitation to be in Mr. Moore's *advanced* history class. The invitation was extended to me at the end of my junior year. I liked how the word "advanced" rolled off the tongue. It was so much more intellectual than "general." Anyhow, because I wanted a challenge I signed up to take his class during my senior year.

Sometime during the summer before my senior year, I received a note in the mail regarding Mr. Moore's class. He wrote that all the seniors taking his advanced history class were required to read a particular book over the next few weeks and be ready to discuss it the first day of class. I thought to myself, *Who does this guy think he is?* Because I had better things to do over the summer, I decided to drop his class right then and there. I reverted back to my favorite word, "general."

On the first day of school, I attended the general history class. There wasn't much to it, and I liked that. The next day I was sitting in Bible class, goofing off with some of my buddies. In walked Mr. Moore. The rowdy class immediately hushed. We all sat up straight with our eyes fixed on him.

He moved past the sword and shield that hung on the wall and approached our Bible teacher, Pastor Cady. They whispered for a few seconds. None of us students breathed. We nervously awaited the outcome of the brief conversation. To my horror, Mr. Moore turned from Pastor Cady, pointed to me and then to the door.

Just to make sure he wasn't mistaken, I pointed at myself and asked, "Me?" He nodded and headed out. I took a huge gulp and my heart sank. When I got to the door, I looked for Mr. Moore. He had already set off down the hall at a brisk pace. I knew I had better catch up to him if I wanted to live to see tomorrow.

He glared at me and threw a folder in my direction.

He intentionally walked 20 feet in front of me. He walked through one hallway and down the next. He walked all the way to his classroom in the basement. He plopped down at a desk. I decided to follow suit and sat down at a desk near his. He glared at me and threw a folder in my direction. It skidded across the desk, and I caught it before it fell off. He said pointedly, "Kary, this is your academic file that goes all the way back to sixth grade. I want you to give me one good reason why you dropped my advanced history class."

I froze. I didn't know what to say. I didn't have an excuse. I was caught. This guy was good. He had nerves of steel, evidenced in the fact that he didn't look away. He just kept staring at me, his eyes boring a hole right through me. I figured if this teacher pursued me with that much passion, then I had better take his class.

So, I took his advanced history class. I took away from that year much more than facts and dates. I learned from that class one of the most important skills I had ever been taught. I learned how to learn and how to think! The way Mr. Moore taught rivaled Robin William's performance in *Dead Poet's Society*. His love for learning was contagious. When Mr. Moore asked a question, he wasn't satisfied with a simple answer. He wanted to know why you gave that particular answer.

God used Mr. Moore to awaken a deep passion I never knew I had. Buried deep within my soul was an insatiable hunger to learn. The more I learned, the more I knew I didn't know. It was addictive. I realized that prior to my interaction with Mr. Moore, I was committing a major sin. I didn't love God with my mind. Sure I loved Him with my heart, with my soul, and with my strength. But I completely avoided loving Him with my mind. Not only did I fail to bring my mind into submission to the Lord, I simply failed to use my mind at all. Here I was, entrusted by God to steward my mind, but instead, I wasted it most of those years leading up to my last year of high school.

*I was committing a major sin. I didn't love God with my mind.*

Since then, I have made a commitment to be a lifelong learner. It's much more than achieving degrees in higher education. It's a way of life, of filtering the world, of dissecting culture. I no longer consume life. I exegete it.

## A Terrible Thing to Waste

I don't think my experience is all that unique. I think many of us who claim to be followers of Christ fail to use our minds, much less love God with our minds. Our churches are filled with disciples who have surrendered the responsibility of reading and interpreting the Word to professional ministers. The Reformers are probably turning over in their graves with horror because of this tendency.

Os Guinness, in *Fit Bodies Fat Minds*, addresses this head on. "As God has given us minds, we can measure obedience by whether we are loving Him with those minds, and disobedience by whether we are not. Loving God with our minds is not ultimately a question of orthodoxy, but of love. Offering up our minds to God in all our thinking is part of our praise. Anti-intellectualism is quite simply a sin."[1]

We aren't given the option of deciding whether or not studying theology is our "thing." Throughout history there have been tragic times when the church has over-spiritualized issues and dismissed the importance of learning, knowledge, and education. The Great Command, handed down to us by our Lord Jesus Christ, is to love the Lord with all our hearts, souls, and minds. Too often we bypass the whole mind thing. We take the lazy person's route of professed reliance upon the Spirit in order to compensate for our ignorance and unwillingness to worship God with our brains.

## A Brief Church History Lesson

As I examined church history, my conviction for theology grew exponentially. Sprinkled throughout the centuries are examples of believers who had a deep understanding and knowledge of God's Word. As C. Christopher Smith explains in *Water, Faith & Wood*, "The Early Church was more interested in making students—i.e., disciples—than it was in making converts. She did not want to cram the pews full of people ignorant of the Word, but rather she sought out souls that were ready for the long journey of discipleship."[2]

Alexandria, famous for its secular schools long before the birth of Christianity, founded the first school of theology. Alexandria was a cosmopolitan city, flourishing in commerce and the home of the greatest library in the ancient world with more than 700,000 volumes. She combined the religious life of Palestine with the intellectual culture of Greece, which resulted in the establishment of a Christian institution.[3] This school provided the church with educated people able to combat the current heresies of the day. Some think that Apollos, a learned Jew of Alexandria who was mighty in the Scriptures, studied in such a school.

As time passed, hunger for learning grew both inside and outside the church. Education was on the rise, and universities were sprouting up. Along with this, three conflicting views began to emerge about the relationship between theology and the university. One camp saw theology as an obligation of the university. Kant argued that it was in the interest of the state to insist on the presence of theology within the university to ensure control over the future leaders of key social institutions.[4] Theology became the queen of the sciences and was integrated into the very fiber of the university. "In Germany, the traditional four faculties (philosophy, medicine, law, and theology) made up the university."[5]

The second camp, the anti-intellectuals, believed that "'pure religion and consummate learning' are incompatible, since the former rests on faith while the latter rests on questions and arguments." In other words, such proponents saw "academicians as over-intellectualized and under-involved."[6]

A third camp preferred a more organic concept of the university. Erasmus, a proponent of this camp, had some major concerns with both of the first two camps. "Erasmus was very critical of the kind of theology done in the universities of his own day—preferring the freedom of the non-attached scholar and gravitating to small, familial academies."[7] After all, it was debatable whether or not dogmatic theology could be taught within university theological studies.[8] Ironically, Erasmus was also against the anti-intellectuals of his day. He fully affirmed the value of secular disciplines for Christian reflection. He believed that Christians should imitate both the "virtues of the apostles and at the same time the learning of Jerome."[9]

## Mushy Minds

Erasmus was onto something that applies to our situation today as well. Believers in the twenty-first century are often guilty of leaving their faith at the door when they leave the church building. In other words, many disciples have a theology, but how that theology affects the rest of life is anyone's guess.

Many of us are guilty of turning off our brains at distinct times throughout our week. Society wires us to do it. You could say that we're programmed to do it. Let's look at the concept of *amusement* for a moment. Much of our lives is built around amusement. A couple years ago, I was shocked to learn the definition of amusement. "Muse" means to think. The prefix "a" means not. Therefore, "amuse" means not to think. An amusement is something we participate in so that we don't have to think.

*Many disciples have a theology, but how that theology affects the rest of life is anyone's guess.*

We're wired to turn our brains off. George Bernard Shaw recognized this and sarcastically commented, "Most people think only once or twice a year. I have made an international reputation by thinking once or twice a week."[10]

Media is a huge business that plays to the tendency of not thinking. The time when we should be turning our brains on even more is the time most of us drop our guard. We rarely bring the idea of following Jesus into how we consume media. I'm not referring to the blatant programming we shouldn't watch but to the ordinary things that slip right by us. What about the worldview behind the commercials we watch? How do the images that appear on our home page attempt to shape us in light of a biblical framework? Discipleship is just as much a part of these things as it is of sermons, worship songs, and prayer services.

I think Satan is thrilled when our minds devolve into mush. It's in the mind where Satan wages his fiercest battles. Scripture warns us to destroy speculations and every lofty thing raised up against the knowledge of God and to take every thought captive to the obedience of Christ.[11]

I believe that mushy minds are even more common today than in the first century. Today we are hit with a preposterous number of mind-shaping thoughts, ideas, and ads. Google announces on its website that the average American is exposed to more than 3,000 ads every day.[12] If we've not developed our minds to be sharp, biblically sound, and theologically framed, we're in tremendous danger. The mind is the gateway where thoughts are conceived and actions are set in motion. Gordon MacDonald expands on this phenomenon of the mind in greater detail:

> In our pressurized society, people who are out of shape mentally usually fall victim to ideas and systems that are destructive to the human spirit and to the human relationship. They are victimized because they have not taught themselves how to think, nor have they set themselves to the lifelong pursuit of growth of the mind. Not having the faculty of a strong mind, they grow dependent upon the thoughts and opinions of others. Rather than deal with ideas and issues, they reduce themselves to lives full of rules, regulations, and programs.[13]

## Lord of All

It's been said that Jesus is either Lord of all, or He is not Lord at all. If following Jesus doesn't affect the way we mow our lawn, the manner in which we view our sexuality, and the way that we treat our neighbor, then I don't want any part of it. Following Jesus is not a little compartment of our lives reduced to a couple hours on Sunday morning. Neither is it a religion bound to the walls of a church building. Erasmus understood this and distinguished himself by stating, "Whereas Socrates brought philosophy down from heaven to earth; I have brought it even into the games, informal conversations, and drinking parties."[14]

Our world once understood this and our educational system was structured around it. Some would argue that the times when our society progressed most rapidly were the times when theology was integrated into the very fiber of education. Educational disciplines didn't stand in isolation from each other. Rather, they all bowed their knees to theology, the queen of the sciences. "As the queen of the sciences, theology's place in the university among the sciences was once assured."[15]

People were not scientists or musicians or astronomers. They were first Christians. Out of their theology they became experts in their fields. Their biblical worldview didn't slow them down or force them to commit intellectual suicide. Quite the contrary, their theology allowed them to exegete and contextualize their world in proper perspective.

*Their theology allowed them to exegete and contextualize their world in proper perspective.*

Theology was more than a set of beliefs requiring practical application. "It was seen as a holistic enterprise that integrally touched all aspects of the faith-directed life."[16] Theology was not only integrated into the hard sciences, but also into culture and art. Educators understood that humanity benefited as a whole "when the treatment of the arts was considered a necessary part of the tasks of constructing theology, interpreting faith and culture, and preparing for the practice of ministry in effect."[17] Thus, theology was a part of all of life, just as all of life was a part of theology.

Art should neither be exempt from our concept of God nor from our theology. God created art. He didn't have to use color, but He did. He didn't have to create taste, but He did. I would venture to say that the world is God's canvas to woo us to Him. Just like a masterpiece brings glory to the artist, so God's handiwork causes us to approach Him with wonder.

Humanism shouldn't have the corner on the arts, but it often does. That is our fault. We're guilty of creating a division within Christendom. We have categorized activities into sacred and secular. Christians are taught that praying and reading the Bible are spiritual exercises. We're also taught that baking a cake, painting a house, and having a vocation other than as a pastor or chaplain is secular. Where did we get this theology?

Most of us have eliminated artists from the church. Of course it's not a blatant expulsion. It's much more subtle. We often place emphasis upon the visible roles within the church, like preaching, teaching, or leading worship. But God used the arts in Scripture.[18] At times He gave artists special gifting, so they could have a viable role within the spiritual life of His people.[19]

It is dangerous to create categories within Christianity. It may be easier when everything is black and white, but we will be much poorer when we prevent God and theology from interfacing with all of life. "A theology that fails to take the arts seriously is an impoverished theology."[20]

What does a biblical theology that incorporates the arts look like? What are some practical outcomes? Wilson Yates, in *The Arts in Theological Education*, gives us some ideas:

> The arts can serve theology as a source in identifying and understanding the religious questions of human existence. The arts can serve theology as a source for understanding the spiritual character of a particular culture. The arts can serve theology as a source of prophetic judgment and protest against human injustice and idolatry.[21]

As we acknowledge that following Jesus touches all facets of life, including the arts, we begin to understand the holistic idea of discipleship. This is *the* model, the *only* model of discipleship presented in the Book of James and the rest of the New Testament. According to the Hebrew mind-set, education is holistic, centered in and through the family, and essentially religious.[22]

## For One and for All

During the Reformation when people were converted, they immediately began a lifelong journey of theological study, regardless of what their professions might be. The new Christians were encouraged to remain in their current places of employment and minister from platforms of good life skills and deep theological conviction.

Today we have reduced the responsibility of theology to the professional minister. Yet Scripture calls every believer a minister. Theology, therefore, is the responsibility of every disciple of Jesus. "Theological education is not a higher stage of Christian education, but a dimension of everyone's Christian education."[23] We do the church and the world a disservice when we farm out theology to the clergy. Oswald Chambers explains in *My Utmost for His Highest*:

> Theology is the responsibility of every Christian. Many people have been duped into thinking that theology is only relevant for the professional minister. This couldn't be farther from the truth. In regard to authentic disciples, God will not make us think like Jesus. We have to do it ourselves; we have to bring every thought into captivity to the obedience of Christ.[24]

In the early church, theology was not seen as a discipline for a select few. As an outgrowth of Judaism, the New Testament affirms that both learning and teaching should be the concern of every Christian. Theology was a lifelong pursuit that required time and effort. "Thus thinking Christianly is inevitably moment by moment, question by question, issue by issue, point by point, and thought by thought."[25] Theology was the deep reservoir from which all of life flowed. Theology wasn't a fragmented academic discipline. On the contrary, it was integrated with every aspect of life.

Theology wasn't a fragmented academic discipline. On the contrary, it was integrated with every aspect of life.

Presently, many churches do not take learning seriously. They merely transmit sermons and expect their parishioners to be formed in a deeply theological way. Robert E. Webber, in *Ancient-Future Faith*, writes, "The church is called to pass down the faith not just in creeds but as a living example."[26] That was the pattern in the early church. As time has marched on, however, much of the church has forgotten it. The "knowledge-based spiritual formation of the 20th century has so reduced the call of Jesus to right belief that many become confused about why mere profession of belief does not bring about life change."[27]

Churches must be more than mere proponents of morality. Do-goodism rejects the core of Christian ethics that "grows out of the redemptive work of Christ."[28] The heart of the biblical message is regeneration. The stories of Israel and Jesus both reflect the prophetic call for everyone to be "a new person within the community of God's people on earth."[29] If Christianity is reduced to the assent of doctrines and creeds without the call for a change of life, Christianity becomes powerless. "The Church should be inspired to rethink its commitment to a program of Christian education which is serious in its goal of learning. Too often the Church's attitude towards learning amounts to a little more than passive satisfaction with its seemingly superficial Sunday scanning of the Scriptures."[30]

For some, the "postmodern moment" has initiated a paradigm shift in the way theological education is perceived. Some churches are switching their loyalties from a Greek mind-set of theological education to a Hebrew concept. In recent years there has been a growing consensus that to create more theologically-trained leaders, there must be a redefinition of who should be theologically trained. Jeff Reed of BILD International states, "It is a biblical idea that 'provides a philosophy and a framework for solving the worldwide problem of a lack of leaders…for returning serious ordered learning to every believer.'"[31]

Marvin R. Wilson explains about the Hebrew concept of everyone and everything being theological: "To the Hebrew mind, everything is theological. That is, the Hebrews made no distinction between the sacred and the secular areas of life. They see all of life as unity. It is all God's domain."[32]

According to the Hebrew concept, clergy received no higher accolades than any other people. All people were theologians regardless of their professions. All people were to be theologically trained, because all people were called to holiness in life.

The Jews understood the all-encompassing view that every person was to be theologically trained. The early church understood that too, and for some, the present postmodern worldview is initiating a return to that understanding. The days of the elite expert are disappearing. Certainly, people are wired differently. Not everyone will thrive in personal study and practical theology. However, the church is returning to the understanding that all believers are ministers and continuing education for ministry is a lifelong process. Regardless of the church's changing view throughout history, the Bible has always seen every believer as a minister.

The essence of theological training is not a piece of paper or a degree on the wall. It is a way of life, expected of every believer. "Theology is neither an academic subject nor a set of beliefs, but a form of divine wisdom accessible to all people as they seek to live out their faith in a concrete way."[33] This Hebrew mind-set, which is also a biblical mind-set, is changing the way theological training is perceived. Obviously, if one believes theological training is intended only for an elite remnant, it will affect the way that training will be conducted. Yet, because of the resurgence of this Hebrew mind-set, significantly initiated by a postmodern worldview, people are rethinking theological training.

## No Theological Robots Allowed

Another thinking trap is to promote a closed approach regarding theology. Certainly there is orthodoxy. Yet, too many Christians never question what they believe. There is truth in Walter Lippmann's statement, "When all think alike, no one thinks very much."[34] That might be one reason we have seen a plethora of young adults exiting the church. The younger generation often perceives the older generation presenting static doctrine. Theology often seems "dead" because it's separate from practice as well as active thinking.

In regard to theological education, Parker Palmer presents a challenge:

> View the classroom as a context for creating a particular culture, a culture of teaching and learning that encourages personal as well as academic formation. Make the classroom a safe place that encourages the fullest participation of students in the learning process. Encourage the expression of feelings, doubts, and dilemmas as well as ideas relating to life and service. Allow our passion for and response to the truth to inform the way we teach and relate to students. Cultivate the possibility of students practicing obedience to the truth inside as well as outside the classroom.[35]

Unless people are allowed to question and wrestle with their faith, "the education given can make no claim to be really Christian at its root because it does not shape perception and impart wisdom."[36] Many churches "want their people to show up for church, to support the budget, and do nothing publicly immoral or disruptive."[37] There is more to "equipping of the saints for the work of service" than merely conforming to behavioral expectations.

I had the privilege of overseeing the youth in my church for five years. Our meetings were much more than disseminating doctrine. Instead, we wrestled with theology. We embraced tension-laced passages. We looked for attributes of God that stretched our thinking. We voiced our concerns. We verbalized our disagreements. Theology wasn't a static exercise. Rather, our community experienced transformation as we experienced Jesus within the text. We didn't read the Bible; we let the Bible read us. After all, is the Bible living and active, or is it dead and impotent?

Sometimes I voiced my frustration with the text. The youth had given me permission to work out my theology. Isn't this what sanctification is all about? Aren't we commanded to work out our salvation with fear and trembling? Of course I come to the Bible with humility. I don't interpret Truth; Truth interprets me. But this is the process. Jesus asked His Father to sanctify us with Truth. Then He said, "Your word is Truth."[38]

*Working out our theology isn't fixed. We all have questions.*

Working out our theology isn't fixed. We all have questions. Yet when we allow an environment that forbids questions and discussion, we obstruct the Spirit.

When I was the Pastor of Student Ministries, our church website had the following statement in the Student Ministries section:

> In our Student Ministries young adults are challenged to make the faith their own. They are encouraged to be thinking followers of Christ that choose to interface with their world.
>
> We believe that just as Jesus entrusted His disciples with the future of Christianity, so our youth should be entrusted with real ministry. Too many people take a "safe" mediocre approach towards spiritual things. They align themselves with a "politically correct" view of Jesus. We encourage students to take a passionate stance for or against the claims that the Bible makes about God, life, and eternity.[39]

I don't think many youth ministries encourage their "*students to take a passionate stance for or against the claims that the Bible makes about God, life, and eternity.*" Yet, "Is there any other way?" Christ encouraged His disciples to make up their minds about Him. He promoted an open atmosphere that allowed for questions. Jesus guided the discussion, but He allowed them to make the faith their own.

A strict environment that merely disseminates doctrine often has shallow disciples. That is the outcome when people don't feel safe enough to voice questions or concerns. If we're honest, at times we all have doubts.

At one of our youth retreats, after a time of intense singing and teaching, we opened the program for the young adults to share. Many people testified about God's faithfulness. Some cried and confessed sin. It was a special session for everyone. As our time was winding down, one teen walked up to the front of the group and said simply, "I can't find God. I've tried and I just can't." Then he sat down. I didn't know how to respond. I approached him privately and asked if he'd like to talk further. He agreed. He went on to tell me about all his doubts. I simply listened. I let him work out his theology, or lack thereof.

What happened? Honestly, not much. Yet, I'll tell you what didn't happen. None of the teens judged this guy. We didn't cram the Bible down his throat. We didn't tell him he couldn't say such things. After all, if people aren't allowed to wrestle with their faith inside the walls of the church, where can they?

Trust me. I had been working with this teen for four years. He knew the answers. Yet, he was still on his journey of believing the Answer. And that is okay. I'd rather have him voice his doubts. I'd rather know where he stands than have him give me a lame performance of religiosity. I believe this teen will be stronger in his faith because he is honestly wrestling with it.

Too often we try to relieve people's tension with God. It's like we feel the need to defend Him or something. Rather than encouraging people to acknowledge their tension and go to God with it, we stand in their way and try to alleviate it. I don't know about you, but my times of greatest growth have been when people left me with my questions and merely pointed me to the One who could handle them. By giving me permission to voice my doubts, they allowed me to process what was really going on inside. And in reality, that was much of the answer.

*Too often we try to relieve people's tension with God.*

## Why We Need to Do Theology

In the end, theology must be a component within every true disciple's life. Theology isn't reduced to a class or a degree.

Rather, it is a way of life. Theology is a framework by which we discern and digest our world. Sadly though, within today's church it's too often absent. Edward Farley explains the current dilemma by asking some fundamental questions:

> Why is it that the vast majority of Christian believers remain largely unexposed to Christian learning—to historical-critical studies of the Bible, to the content and structures of the great doctrines, to two thousand years of classic works on the Christian life, to the basic disciplines of theology, biblical languages, and Christian ethics? Why do bankers, lawyers, farmers, physicians, homemakers, scientists, salespeople, managers of all sorts, people who carry out all kinds of complicated tasks in their work and home, remain at a literalist, elementary school level in their religious understanding? How is it that high school age church members move easily and quickly into the complex world of computers, foreign languages, DNA, calculus, and cannot even make a beginning in historical-critical interpretation of a single text of Scripture? How is it possible one can attend or even teach in a Sunday school for decades and at the end of that time lack the interpretive skills of someone who has taken three or four weeks in an introductory course in the Bible at a university or seminary?[40]

Farley raises interesting questions. Yet such is the reality when we farm out theology to the professional minister. This phenomenon isn't simply a recent trend. It seems it occurred in the first century as well.

> *The brethren immediately sent Paul and Silas away by night to Berea, and when they arrived, they went into the synagogue of the Jews. Now these were more noble-minded than those in Thessalonica, for they received the word with*

*great eagerness, examining the Scriptures daily to see whether these things were so.*

Acts 17:10-11

Notice that the Bible distinguishes between the Thessalonicans and the Bereans. The Bereans didn't take what they heard at face value. Instead, they searched the Scriptures. They compared what they heard with the written Word. The writer of Acts complimented them. These people "owned" their faith because they wrestled with it. As a result, they probably were much deeper disciples than the Thessalonicans who simply digested what they heard without even chewing on it.

Many disciples focus only on loving God with their hands instead of with their heads as well. The church must be filled with more than just nice people. It is not supposed to be only what we do that makes us different from the world, but also what we know. Certainly other faiths "do" ministry. They love each other and care for the poor and the sick. The church needs people who minister out of a deep theology. It needs disciples who balance their knowing with their doing.

We can't forget to do our theology either. Theology that fails to have skin on it is a failed theology. It is the responsibility of every believer to live out what he or she believes. Otherwise, as we saw earlier, we don't really believe it. Robert Banks exhorts, "Students must develop the capacity to do theology themselves rather than simply learning theology or how theologians go about it."[41]

Theology that fails to have skin on it is a failed theology.

There is a step, however, that comes before doing our theology, and that brings us to our second component. Upon knowing our theology, our first component, we must then *become* our theology. Perhaps a better way of saying this is that we must embody our theology. As *being* is the second measurement of discipleship, spiritual formation is its second component.

# Spiritual Formation

*The people of God are called to be today what*
*the world is called to be ultimately.*
John Yoder

The anti-drug commercial of the eighties taught us that nobody ever says, "I want to be a junkie when I grow up." Likewise, nobody ever says, "I want to be unsuccessful when I grow up." So in our discussion of discipleship, if we want to avoid being unsuccessful, we must first understand the biblical definition of success. Success as a disciple has everything to do with the second component of our paradigm, spiritual formation.

> *This book of the law shall not depart from your mouth, but you shall meditate on it day and night, so that you may be careful to do according to all that is written in it; for then you will make your way prosperous, and then you will have success.*
> Joshua 1:8

This verse suggests that success is somehow tied to meditating on God's Word. I've often wondered what it means to meditate. Most of us have the mental picture of a guy doing yoga or chanting. Call me simplistic, but I have a different picture of what meditation means.

Think back to a time when you walked through the food section at a carnival or theme park. You probably saw vendors selling hot dogs, nachos, and powdered sugar elephant ears. Often, there is also a vendor selling taffy. What does the vendor do to keep his taffy from hardening and becoming unusable? He positions the taffy on rotating metal prongs that continually weave in and out. The taffy is suspended, stretched back and forth, over and over again. As a result, it remains pliable and moldable until it's ready to be consumed.

That is what I think meditation is all about. It's a process that prevents us from becoming hardened and unusable. It keeps us pliable and moldable. It's a position in which we willingly place ourselves. We entrust ourselves to God, and He stretches us over and over again until we're ready to be consumed.

We can meditate on specific passages in the Bible. We can meditate on God's miracles or His faithfulness in our lives. We can meditate on the parables of Christ or the Acts of the Apostles. Although the specific subject may change, the process doesn't. Meditation on the Word is necessary if we are to be successful in spiritual formation.

Meditation and spiritual formation go hand in hand. Spiritual formation has been the buzzword of the last couple decades within churches and seminaries across the country. We often talk about it, but what does it mean? Spiritual formation is simply the process of being formed spiritually.

Spiritual formation was the Apostle Paul's burning passion for himself and for the believers in the churches that he started. It was to that end he labored. He described spiritual formation as a birth process.

> *My dear children, for whom I am again in the pains of childbirth until Christ is formed in you.*
>
> Galatians 4:19, NIV

The childbirth process is not a walk in the park. When my wife gave birth to our first child, she did an excellent job. But it was neither a speedy nor a painless process. It took tremendous energy. They don't call it "labor" for nothing. Although tremendous pain is involved, the joy on the other side is often beyond comprehension.

Paul used childbirth language when he addressed the Galatians about their spiritual formation. He called them his children. He spoke about the pain involved. But don't forget the outcome. The joy on the other side was that Christ was formed within them.

Why is it so important for God's people to undergo continuous spiritual transformation? Well for starters, "The Bible is all about life change."[1] We need to stop thinking that evangelistic ministry is directed only to the unregenerate. Darrel L. Guder states in *The Continuing Conversion of the Church* that "the New Testament is addressed to believers and it evangelizes at every turning."[2]

> *We need to stop thinking that evangelistic ministry is directed only to the unregenerate.*

In other words, we don't stop being formed spiritually until the day we die, or the day we're raptured. This goes back to our prior discussion about salvation. Believers have been saved; they are being saved; and they will be saved. When we resist spiritual renewal, we're resisting the very hand of God. "Life is a constant process of deaths and rebirths."[3] The ultimate death is when we refuse to change. Regeneration is the first and ultimate rebirth, but renewal is rebirth as well. We have the potential for rebirth as long as we hold an open hand out to God and the sanctifying process that He desires to continue within us.

## What Spiritual Formation Is

There is much confusion surrounding the topic of spiritual formation. What is it?

1) Spiritual formation is a death of sorts. Death is the crux of discipleship. Jesus said to His disciples, "If anyone wishes to come after Me, he must deny himself, and take up his cross daily and follow Me."[4] This daily death is not often a literal death, although sometimes it might be. More often, it's a death of self, of habits, of addictions, of prejudices, and of rights. As we die to self, we live to Christ. This is the slow process of Christ being formed within us.

2) Spiritual formation is transformation. "In the Bible the final goal of God's saving intention is the transformation of all creation."[5] When believers fail to be transformed, inevitably we will fail to transform our world. We can't lead people where we have not willingly ventured ourselves. We can't expect to evoke renewal on a global level when we resist spiritual renewal on a personal level.

The church is to be the witness and example of what it means to be the people of God. Our witness is discounted when the church fails to be transformed in her being. Likewise, the church's transformation in her being brings credibility to her message. Transformation isn't easy. It "has a very real cost, but so does failure to change."[6]

*When believers fail to be transformed, inevitably we will fail to transform our world.*

Perhaps we reject transformation because our natural tendency is to reject conflict. Transformation often involves conflict, or at the very minimum, it involves tension. "Without tension there is no energy, without energy there is no movement, and without movement there is no progress."[7] Just as working out our theology involves tension, so does working out our spirituality. Essentially, discipleship is a process laced with tension. That isn't a bad thing. Too often we equate harmony with godliness. We aren't called to be harmonious. We're called to be disciples. Discipleship isn't for the faint of heart. Jesus told us, "The kingdom of heaven has been forcefully advancing, and forceful men lay hold of it."[8]

## What Spiritual Formation Is Not

Just as important regarding the topic of spiritual formation is to examine what it is not. 1) Spiritual formation is not a program. "Spiritual life is a living thing; it's not mechanical. The soul will not be manipulated like a thermostat or turned on and off like a switch."[9] Our microwave culture desires immediate spirituality. We're consumed with anything that promises instant spiritual transformation.[10]

2) Spiritual formation isn't easy. When we present salvation like it's a walk in the park, we're doing people a disservice. I don't think we should present it as if it were an extreme sport, with life-threatening danger and intense blood, sweat, and tears. But neither should we present salvation like it's a three-minute prayer. Jesus told people that if they weren't ready to make major adjustments, they shouldn't sign up.

> *If anyone comes to Me, and does not hate his own father and mother and wife and children and brothers and sisters, yes, and even his own life, he cannot be My disciple. Whoever does not carry his own cross and come after Me cannot be My disciple. For which one of you, when he wants to build a tower, does not first sit down and calculate the cost, to see if he has enough to complete it? Otherwise, when he has laid a foundation, and is not able to finish, all who observe it begin to ridicule him, saying, 'This man began to build and was not able to finish.'*
>
> *Or what king, when he sets out to meet another king in battle, will not first sit down and consider whether he is strong enough with ten thousand men to encounter the one coming against him with twenty thousand? Or else, while the other is still far away, he sends a delegation and asks for terms of peace. So then, no one of you can be My disciple who does not give up all his own possessions.*
>
> Luke 14:26-33

In both illustrations, Jesus said to count the cost before we decide to be His disciples. Salvation is free; we don't do a thing for it. If we have to work for it then it's no longer by grace. Salvation, however, isn't a one-time event either. It's a way of life. It's a lifelong journey. For disciples, every minute of every day can and should be lived through the power of Christ. Discipleship isn't striving in the flesh. It's abiding in the Spirit.

Discipleship isn't striving in the flesh. It's abiding in the Spirit.

## Pushing Through the Plateau

Theology (our first component) and spiritual formation (our second component) are intrinsically linked. "Practical theology finally concerns the formation of human selves."[11] Spiritual formation is the embodiment of our theology. It's good to know the Bible and to memorize it. But unless a disciple is able to interpret biblical facts, apply the knowledge, and ultimately know God in a deeper way, the message is missed.[12] This is a shift from where we have been. In the past it was thought that the most effective way to deepen a person's spiritual life was to know God's Word better. In reality, the most effective way to deepen one's spiritual life is to know God better. People can know God's Word, but fail to know God.

Many disciples reach a plateau in their spirituality. They become stuck in a routine and feel they're just going through the motions. In the context of spiritual formation, to know God better we must give up control. Robert E. Quinn explains, "Deep change means surrendering control. Making a deep change involves abandoning and 'walking into the land of uncertainty.'"[13] The first step is to stand before God in the nakedness of our sinful selves.[14]

I believe salvation is essentially surrendering control. Sometimes people present salvation as inviting Jesus to be one's co-pilot. I've seen Christian bumper stickers that say, *My co-pilot is a Jewish carpenter* or *God's not dead, he's still alive, he's my co-pilot!* There is nothing "co-" about discipleship. It's not like we sit in the airplane cockpit of our lives debating with Jesus about where we should travel. He wants to go to California. We want to go to New York. So we settle on a compromise and go to Kansas instead. This is foolishness, yet sadly it is often the case for many of us. Discipleship means *following* Jesus. It's not walking alongside Jesus, nor is it leading Jesus. We need to label such theology for what it is, heresy.

Of course, we're involved in the process of discipleship. But we are not calling the shots. We don't split the decision-making responsibility with Jesus 50-50. Believers do have a responsibility. Sanctification is a two-way street. We dare not sit around and wait for spiritual formation to fall upon us. We need to engage the Spirit actively through our prayers and petitions. "Individuals can posture themselves to experience the presence and power of God in their lives."[15]

## The Posture of Prayer

The key that unlocks the door to spiritual formation is prayer. I'll be honest with you. I'm not one of those superheroes of the faith who wakes up and spends an hour in uninterrupted prayer on a daily basis. I'm not even close to that, but I'm sure some of you are and for that I applaud you.

There are thousands of saints more qualified to speak about prayer than I am. I've read their writings. Every time I do, I get excited, but also a little discouraged. I've never been able to come close to their prayer habits. But I too am on the journey of discipleship, and it is a journey. I certainly haven't arrived yet, and I ask for your grace as I tell you about some of my thoughts and patterns concerning prayer.

First, I believe prayer isn't an event we experience, but a posture we take. Although I don't spend great lengths of time in undisrupted prayer, I do try to maintain a constant posture of prayer. The Scriptures exhort us to pray without ceasing. If prayer were simply an event, then this command would be impossible to achieve. No one can pray at all times and forever avoid eating, going to the bathroom, and sleeping. But prayer is much more than an event. On many levels it's like breathing. "As we breathe unceasingly, that breathing supports life and renews our corporeal system. As we develop our ability to pray unceasingly with the breath of prayer, God's love and life will support and renew us."[16] Prayer is not an activity we do or service we attend. Prayer ought to be as natural as the air we breathe.

Prayer opens the heart of God and fills our empty souls.[17] It is the verbalization of deep longing and passion. In *The Principles and Practice of Prayer*, Ivan H. French explains, "Prayer is an expression of instinctive desire... [It is] communion with God. ...Prayer is petition. ...Prayer is the expression of...dependence. ...[It is] conflict with Satan."[18]

When we see prayer as a posture, we're more easily able to incorporate it into our lives. When it's perceived as a posture, we can be in prayer wherever we are and whatever we're doing. Prayer is essentially dependence. It's saying, "I can't do it on my own, but I know Who can."

Obviously, the Son of God needed no convincing that prayer was essential to all of life. Jesus said, "The Son can do nothing of Himself, unless it is something He sees the Father doing; for whatever the Father does, these things the Son also does in like manner."[19] Yet, many of us go for days or weeks without any expressed dependence upon God. We live life on cruise control, and only when we hit a bump, do we enter a mind-set of prayer.

A life of prayer is hard to model and even harder to measure. It is personal and private; therefore, a life without prayer can often go undetected—at least for a while. However, if we consistently fail to live a life of prayer, we'll always be shallow disciples.

## Obstacles to Prayer

There are many obstacles to prayer. Perhaps one reason we don't pray is that we fail to see our need for it. Perhaps we don't see our need for prayer because we have a high view of ourselves and a low view of God. We think we're better off than we really are. We rationalize that we can accomplish a lot merely by relying on the strength of the flesh. I believe if we could only get a glimpse of what God can do through us when fully yielded to Him, we'd never live another day in our own strength.

> *Perhaps we don't see our need for prayer because we have a high view of ourselves and a low view of God.*

Another obstacle to prayer is that many of us feel we can't be honest with God. We believe our prayers must be sanctified. In reality, God wants us to come to Him just as we are. To think that we can come to Him all cleaned up is to imagine that another source, other than God, can purify us. We must come to Him exactly as we are, whether we're dirty, broken, or bruised.

God isn't impressed with religious prayers that hide who we really are and how we really feel. Think about it. David was a man after God's own heart. Have you ever looked at David's prayers? Many of them don't seem that spiritual. Some of his prayers cause theologians to squirm. They classify those prayers as the Imprecatory Psalms. In them, David says some pretty mean, unspiritual, and downright seemingly sinful things. Consider Psalm 109:1-15.



> *O God of my praise, Do not be silent! For they have opened the wicked and deceitful mouth against me; They have spoken against me with a lying tongue. They have also surrounded me with words of hatred, And fought against me without cause. In return for my love they act as my accusers; But I am in prayer. Thus they have repaid me evil for good, And hatred for my love. Appoint a wicked man over him, And let an accuser stand at his right hand. When he is judged, let him come forth guilty, And let his prayer become sin. Let his days be few; Let another take his office. Let his children be fatherless And his wife a widow. Let his children wander about and beg; And let them seek sustenance far from their ruined homes. Let the creditor seize all that he has, And let strangers plunder the product of his labor. Let there be none to extend lovingkindness to him, Nor any to be gracious to his fatherless children. Let his posterity be cut off; In a following generation let their name be blotted out. Let the iniquity of his fathers be remembered before the LORD, And do not let the sin of his mother be blotted out. Let them be before the LORD continually, That He may cut off their memory from the earth.*

David prayed that his enemies' wives would become widows and that their children would become fatherless. If this wasn't bad enough, in Psalm 69:28 David asked the Lord to blot out his enemies from the book of life. He prayed that they might not be recorded with the righteous. Cutting to the chase, David prayed that God would send his enemies to hell. Where is the "love your enemies" thing that Jesus preached about?

Remember though, David was a man after God's own heart. Either God lied about what he thought of David, or else there is something intrinsically spiritual about being real with God.

I think God can deal with our anger, our frustration, and our humanity. But I don't think God can deal with us when we're fake, because then we never see our own need for Him.

David didn't act out these prayers in the Imprecatory Psalms. He was talking to God. However, in his conversation he was real about how he felt. David didn't stand up in front of all Israel and preach this type of prayer. Yet I'm glad that God included them in the Bible in addition to the comforting ones that we often read. It gives me hope because I'm often like David. I struggle with similar rage, passion, and revenge. And like David, I share them with God. This is what spiritual formation is all about.

*If we ever hope to be followers of Jesus with our being, then we must be honest about where we are.*

If we ever hope to be followers of Jesus with our being, then we must be honest about where we are. That is why Jesus was so opposed to the Pharisees. They presented themselves as better than they really were. Because they were proud of their state, God couldn't form Himself inside them. They didn't see their need for Him.

Jesus addressed this issue in the Beatitudes. He said, "Blessed are the poor in spirit, for theirs is the kingdom of heaven."[20] The term "poor in spirit" actually means spiritually bankrupt. The Greek word *ptōchŏs* speaks about someone who crouches and cowers in a beggarly fashion. Jesus is saying that the kingdom of heaven belongs to those who perceive themselves as spiritually desperate and bankrupt. That is because it is only when we see our need that we can invite the Spirit to form Himself within us.

## Walking in the Spirit

Perhaps you've heard the phrase "walking in the Spirit." Scripture tells us that if we walk in the Spirit, we'll no longer carry out the desires of the flesh. This verse is closely related to spiritual formation. Not carrying out the desires of the flesh has much to do with being spiritually formed.

I remember meditating some time ago on the concept of walking in the Spirit. I had no idea what it meant. I talked to a few ministry leaders I knew and read a couple books on the concept. I received many different thoughts about what it meant. I think we often make it more complicated than it is.

*Pĕripatĕō* is the Greek word for walk. It refers to living, conducting oneself, or leading a life. In other words, if we conduct ourselves or live our lives by the Spirit, we won't carry out the lusts of the flesh. The next verse in Galatians reveals more about the relationship between the flesh and the Spirit.

> *For the flesh sets its desire against the Spirit, and the Spirit against the flesh; for these are in opposition to one another, so that you may not do the things that you please.*
>
> Galatians 5:17

The flesh and the Spirit are warring against each other. There is a war going on inside every disciple. The two natures are battling it out. Our flesh wants to have us carry out its desires. Even though part of us wants to do the Spirit's will, the flesh seeks to trump that divine desire.

Every day of our lives we must make a choice. That is what spiritual formation is all about. Will we say yes to the Spirit or to the flesh? We will overcome the flesh only if we conduct our lives by the Spirit. Walking in the Spirit goes back to the whole dependence issue again. Most days, I try to wake up and intentionally have an honest dialogue with myself. I tell myself, *Kary, today you're capable of any sin. You'll fall into those sins if you don't rely upon the Spirit's strength.*

Some might call me a fatalist on the basis of this private conversation I have with myself. I call myself a realist. The truth is that just because I've been a follower of Christ for years, just because I'm a pastor, just because I know the Bible—all of that isn't enough. I still have a fleshly side that longs to consume me. At any moment it can and will if I fail to live my life in dependence upon the Spirit.

I still have a fleshly side that longs to consume me.

## It's Worth It

With all this talk about the work, the effort, and the energy that it takes to be spiritually formed, you might wonder if it's worth it. I believe it's not only worth it, but it's also necessary.

Many people enjoyed the *Rocky* movies (all 57 of them). Each one of those movies, along with nearly every other movie about a champion or competitor, has one common factor. The hero has to undergo intense, rigorous training to beat his opponent. Is it any different in the spiritual realm? If we're going to be formed in a new way, it takes intentional effort. Note how Paul refers to the spiritual formation process.

> *Therefore I run in such a way, as not without aim; I box in such a way, as not beating the air; but I discipline my body and make it my slave, so that, after I have preached to others, I myself will not be disqualified.*
>
> 1 Corinthians 9:26-27

Paul made his body his slave. He conducted his life with intentionality. He didn't want to be disqualified.

No one competes in the Olympics without undergoing rigorous training. No one shows up without a burning desire to win. Yet, we often approach discipleship in a casual manner. We have a "take-it-or-leave-it" approach. Where is our burning passion to be spiritually formed? I think we need to find our courage. We need to stop playing small.

In his book *In Ordinary Time*, Robert C. Bondi challenges, "We have to be willing to be stubborn and persistent with God. In fact, we'll have to be exactly like the widow with the unjust judge, and Jacob wrestling the angel for a blessing."[21] Jacob wasn't timid, even in his dealings with God. He had a "never-say-die" approach. Too often we talk to God like, "If it's not too much trouble" or "I know you're really busy but…" There have been times when I've been so desperate for an answer, a sign, or a request that I've told God "I'm not getting up off my knees until You speak to me." Some might see this as disrespect, but I don't think it is.

There is a concept related to prayer that very few disciples know about. It's called importunity. Webster defines importunate as "troublesomely urgent or overly persistent in request or demand."[22] Importunity is the perfect word to describe the widow in Luke 18. The Bible says that Jesus taught this parable in order to "show that at all times they ought to pray and not to lose heart (v. 1)." Importunity is the concept Jesus is getting at and the posture we should try to emulate in our prayer lives.

Prayer is a major key to being formed spiritually, and spiritual formation is a necessary component of authentic discipleship. Without it, we'll fail to be followers of Jesus with our being, and it will be much more difficult for Him to use us.

> Spiritual formation helps move one's ministry maturation process beyond a focus on skills and knowledge to a being base. Until the Lord has shaped the vessel, it will not serve His purpose.[23]
>
> Edgar J. Elliston and J. Timothy Kauffman

# Ministry

*The great end of life is not knowledge, but action.*
T.H. Huxley

That summer evening I was ready, or at least I tried to convince myself I was. I drove to my first lesson intentionally listening to testosterone-enhancing music. I needed any edge I could get. I got out of my car and walked to my doom with ice water and duffle bag in hand. Who was I fooling?

I did have a couple things going for me. I had spent the week in intensive study. I was glad my friend bought me the book. It was a thick manual that covered the basics and more. It had a couple hundred pictures with step-by-step moves. I'll admit it, I was terribly nervous. But knowing that I had reviewed the pictures again and again gave me a little bit of confidence.

I walked into the jiu-jitsu club feeling like a third grader ready to meet the dentist. The worst thing about being a rookie in jiu-jitsu is that everybody knows. If you've ever done any form of martial arts, you know you have to wear a belt that identifies your rank. Sure enough, as I walked to the back of the room, past the mats, I saw people wearing many different colored belts. My belt was white. In layman's terms, that translates into "sucker."

I paid my fee to the black belt instructor and then changed into my gi. If jiu-jitsu isn't tough enough, you have to wear what feels like a 20-pound snowsuit.

The students circled around and began to stretch. The summer heat poured into the cramped club. In the corner, one lone fan tried its best to cool off the entire room. I sweated profusely as we jogged around the room. Finally, the instructor told us to pair up and warm up, as if we weren't warm already. He told us to get into a side mount and practice putting our partner into a keylock. Our opponent was to give us 50 percent resistance.

*Keylock*. I had heard that term before. I flipped through the pages of my mind. Got it. Sure enough, I saw the move in my head spread out over eight different pictures. I thought with my opponent at 50 percent resistance it shouldn't be that tough. My first mistake was that I *thought*. My knowledge of the keylock had no effect whatsoever. When it came time to sink the move, I missed it big time. I could tell you all about how to do the move on paper, but when it came to putting it into practice, I was clueless.

## Disciples on Paper

It's no different with discipleship. Many believers can tell you a whole lot about the Bible or Jesus. Such people seem to be disciples on paper. But when it comes to putting it into practice, just like my jiu-jitsu experience, they fail to apply what they know. It's one thing to wax eloquently about something. It's an entirely different thing to embody it and then put it into practice.

If we are authentic disciples, we can be confident that we'll measure up in our knowing, being, doing, and reproducing. Theology, the first component, addresses the need to measure up in our knowing. Spiritual formation, the second component, addresses the need to measure up in our being. And ministry, the third component, addresses the need to measure up in our doing.

> Ministry is the flesh that takes form upon the bones of theology.

Ministry refers to the practical ways of serving incarnated into the life of a disciple. Theology is merely theoretical unless it is lived out. Christ said that if people desire to be great, they must first become servants. Ministry is the flesh that takes form upon the bones of theology. A life without ministry is selfish and hypocritical. A true disciple has passion to minister that flows from a deep theology.

Ministry was often a litmus test in the early church as to whether someone was an authentic disciple. According to Hippolytus' exhortation in *Apostolic Tradition*, if one's life lacked right doing, sacraments, such as baptism, could be withheld:

> When they are chosen who are to receive baptism, let their lives be examined, whether they have lived honorably while catechumens, whether they honored the widows, whether they visited the sick, and whether they have done every good work. If those who bring them forward bear witness for them that they have done so, then let them hear the Gospel.[1]

Neither Jesus nor the Early Church allowed disciples to sit on a hill and study theology at the expense of ministry. Jesus didn't pull His followers away from people for three years, put them in a room, and lecture them, only to send them out on their own with a certificate that testified of their competence. Although Jesus took adequate time instructing His own, He often trained them in the midst of ministering. In *Theologians in Thought and Life*, Ray S. Anderson refers to this process as experiential learning.

> The process involved in experiential learning is the direct opposite of that in information processing. It begins with action, with the immediate experience of the learner. Its objective is not the acquisition of some technical skill. Thus, the essential matter in experiential learning is the movement from the particular experience to conceptualization, to the organization and formulation of theory, principles, or knowledge discerned through reflection on experience.[2]

Learning while in ministry is a natural process. People pay more attention to instruction when they first realize their need for it. For example, I didn't care how to change a baby's diaper until my newborn son was crying because he had a wet diaper. You can bet that I paid close attention to the nurse as she performed this complicated procedure. I watched so that I could do the next one and many other "next ones."

It was the same with my seminary experience. I was not pastoring a church during my first year of seminary. What I learned was great stuff, but for the most part, it was just theoretical. During my second year, however, I was also in full-time vocational ministry. Thus, I listened in a completely different way. It was no longer about grades or papers. I hung on the words of my professors in order to sharpen my ministry skills.

You might say because I was in the midst of ministering, my learning was enhanced. Experts agree. "Learning is enhanced by actively experiencing the content and processes of the area of study, and by reflecting on the meaning of that experience."[3]

That is the pattern Jesus used. First, He taught His disciples.[4] Then, He modeled spiritual formation.[5] Eventually, He sent His disciples out in actual ministry. However, as Luke 10 reveals, when the disciples returned, they reflected immediately upon their experience. That allowed for even more teaching and instruction. Yet it was a different kind of instruction. Now they knew what type of questions to ask because they had lived it. Disciples should set aside a time to develop the mind. Christ's model, however, was much more integrated. It was natural. He taught the disciples, but He also was intentional about having them interact with people.

Learning that sticks tends to be more about doing than knowing. It involves the heart and hands, not just the head. Edgar J. Elliston and J. Timothy Kauffman expound on this in *Developing Leaders for Urban Ministries*.

> "One learns what one does." It's not what the teacher does that provides the learning. Rather it is what the learner does. One will never learn to play a guitar by talking about it. One will never learn to swim without getting in the water. One will not learn to work with dysfunctional

> families where chemical dependency is present without being involved with such families. One will probably not learn to start new churches without doing it.[6]

When ministry is introduced into our lives, we're much closer to the true intent of theological education. We learn in order that we might apply. Theology is the fuel. Spiritual formation is the vehicle. Ministry is the destination. Ray Anderson explains:

*When ministry is introduced into our lives, we're much closer to the true intent of theological education.*

> The primary goal of theological education, as I see it, is the training of persons to learn. This involves the dynamic interaction of theory and practice, of study and experience. It requires the capacity both to discern the theological meaning in the infinite variety of experiences in ministry, and through disciplined study the acquisition of knowledge to enlarge one's capacity to interpret experience. Integration is, I think, the most difficult element in theological education.[7]

## What's My Ministry?

I've often seen a negative trend in newer Christians. I don't blame them. Instead, I'm inclined to blame older believers like myself. Many of us do a poor job of plugging newer Christians into ministry. Think about it. Many new converts have no experience whatever. When they come to Christ, we expect them to have everything figured out, including their talents, spiritual gifts, and direction in ministry.

Instead of taking the time to instruct them about what it means to minister and how to choose an area of ministry, many times we just throw them into random areas. That's one way to do it, but is it the best way?

There is something to be said about getting your feet wet in ministry. I've learned what I'm not good at simply by diving in and trying different tasks. People kindly told me I'm a horrible singer. Thus, I learned quickly that I shouldn't minister in the praise and worship area. To do so would hinder the ministry.

Pastor Tim Boal recently explained to several young leaders in my area how to find one's calling for ministry. He wrote down three terms: desire, ability, and opportunity. When these three things intersect, he suggested, you've probably found your calling for ministry—at least at that point in your life.

In other words, if you have a desire to work with teens, take the opportunity and work with them. Once you've had the opportunity, do you still have the desire? If so, what does your community of faith think? Do they agree that you have the ability to work with teens? If you've sought the Lord and these three things line up, then dive into that ministry.

No model is foolproof. Neither should someone avoid meeting a true need simply because he feels it's not his gift. I remember asking a person to help take the trash to the dumpster after an outreach event. He refused and told me it wasn't his gift. Needless to say, I wasn't impressed.

My advice for new believers is to pray first. Ask God to open your eyes to the needs around you. Sometimes God will give you a special ability to see a need that exists right in front of you. I've had people approach me and ask if they could bridge a gap in an already existing ministry. I've been humbled because often I haven't even recognized these gaps existed. Entire groups of people might have been missed in the process.

> *Ministry is not an activity we sometimes do… It's a lifestyle we live.*

One time we had an outreach event to local teens only because a lady named Vickie and her daughter Emily had the eyes to see a need. They mobilized a dozen others to pitch in so a certain group of teens might see Christ.

The main thing is to get involved. We don't simply *do* ministry. Rather we *are* ministers. That is part of the call of a disciple. Ministry is not an activity we sometimes do. It's not an event we attend. Rather, it's a call we embrace. It's a lifestyle we live.

Ministry is a vital extension of the church. "The Church is to be the expression of the kingdom to the watching world."[8] We are the hands and feet of Jesus here on earth. We can't present a compassionate and caring Lord when we, His church, fail to demonstrate that care and compassion.

## Theology Gets a Bad Name

If theology is not practically applied, it quickly gets a bad name. "Frequently…theological education in the United States has been conceived not as a theological problem, but as a matter of practical application and technique."[9] The monastic life was often accused of sacrificing ministry at the expense of emphasizing theology and spiritual formation. Some monasteries realized this unhealthy behavior and balanced their concept of discipleship by taking ministry seriously. "Theodosius' monastery had a special house for the sick and several others provided holistic care for the poor, including employment."[10]

Essentially what we're talking about is living out the kingdom. It's one thing to teach about the kingdom or say the kingdom exists inside us. It's an entirely different thing to incarnate the kingdom. Doug Pagitt voices his frustration in *Reimagining Spiritual Formation*.

> There is little question in my mind that many of us in the Protestant church have erred in our overemphasis on teaching about Jesus to the exclusion of the call to the Kingdom life. While this is in no way true in every situation, there are far too many times that we allow ourselves to believe that efforts of education about Jesus are the full extent of evangelism and discipleship.[11]

So what does it mean to live out the kingdom? What does it mean to embrace your call as a minister? I think we need to look at the way Christ lived. Jesus, the One who often told us that the kingdom is at hand, was a voice for those who had none. He spoke up for the mute, the lame, and the marginalized. Jesus incarnated the kingdom by living according to a different mind-set. He gave away His life in order to find it. He died that we might live. He embodied peace and conquered entire nations as a result. Jesus brought the kingdom to humanity. He didn't merely preach it.

That is what true ministry is all about. Robert Banks expounds:

> Our thinking should be embodied, experiential, and contextual, not abstract, objective, and universal. The principal characteristics of such praxis are accountability to minority groups, collaborative reflection, lives-in-relation as an epistemological starting point, cultural diversity, and shared commitment to the work of justice."[12]

The apostle James summarized ministry by stating, "Pure and undefiled religion in the sight of our God and Father is this: to visit orphans and widows in their distress, and to keep oneself unstained by the world."[13] As we stop merely *doing* ministry and instead embrace our call to *be* ministers, then we'll be much closer to Jesus' concept of the kingdom.

> The church is called to pass down the faith not just in creeds but as a living example.
>
> Robert Webber

# Coaching

*We need people around us who will tell us what we need to hear as opposed to people who tell us what we want to hear.*
Rick Packer

I was pretty bummed one day. It all started when I ran into someone who started to rip me to shreds. This guy confronted me on all kinds of issues. I take that back. It wasn't confronting. That is too nice a word. It was more like violently accusing. The funny thing is I just listened quietly. I felt like defending myself, but I didn't have the energy. Having a newborn baby in the house and suffering from sleep deprivation, I didn't have the strength to get into an argument. I let him run his mouth and I truly listened.

At the end of our conversation I was pretty torn up. I walked away and started praying. I said, "God is this from you? Maybe this guy is right? Maybe I'm all messed up?" I had four strong emotions come over me all at once. I felt ashamed. I felt confused. I felt afraid. And I felt depressed.

You might be thinking, *Wow, Kary sure is sensitive*. Maybe I am. But words have always been tremendously powerful to me.

I sat on the couch even more drained. I kept rehearsing in my mind this guy's advice over and over again. I wanted to shake it, but I just couldn't. For some strange reason, my friend Chet popped into my mind. I'm not really sure why. He just did.

Chet is an interesting guy. He was my life coach for four years. Chet coaches business executives for a living. This bold believer gets paid to coach CEOs of major corporations all over the world about life, God, and leadership. Needless to say, Chet's a great guy with a great job. He challenged my faith in a completely fresh way. He helped me steer through religion and get to the point.

Anyhow, there I was, sitting on the couch in a state of self-doubt. I was in a desperate prayer mode, just trying to sort out what was truth and what was error. I didn't want to dismiss this guy's advice just because it rubbed me the wrong way. On the other hand, just because someone yelled, screamed, and threw in a few Bible verses didn't mean it was of God either. Needless to say, I was confused.

*...just because someone yelled, screamed, and threw in a few Bible verses didn't mean it was of God either.*

I was thinking about Chet. Five seconds later my cell phone rang. I picked it up, and guess who was on the other line? No joke, it was Chet. What a contrast to the guy who had just ripped me to shreds. We talked for a few minutes. Chet told me he was on the road traveling. I told him about my run-in with the guy. He listened to me talk. He heard my situation. Then God used Chet to speak truth into my life. As he talked, I began to see things in perspective.

When Chet and I were in a coaching relationship he didn't always go easy on me. Often, God used him to call me out when I was being lame or weak. There were many times when he said tough things I didn't want to hear. But he did it in a way that was challenging and not condemning. God put Chet into my life for a season to sharpen me and stretch me to be the person that He created me to be.

Chet isn't the only coach God has blessed me with. My wife Kelly is my coach as well. She challenges me in the areas where I'm weak. I don't always receive her coaching with the most loving attitude. Nonetheless, she has an uncanny ability to speak truth into my life.

I'm humbled that God has given me excellent coaches in every phase of my life. It began in my childhood with my parents. It continued in college and seminary with my mentor, David Plaster. While serving as a pastor, my own pastor, Rick Nuzum, coached me on how to love people and minister to them in their time of crisis. Currently, several other colleagues and friends function as coaches in my life. These are the most precious parts of my life, my coaches.

I'm not a really emotional guy, but I'm almost tearing up right now as I think of how they've stuck with me in the tough times. I am who I am today because of these key people that God allowed to pour into my life. They have the courage to confront me. They have the words to console me. And they have the time to challenge me.

## Fourth and Final

Coaching is the fourth and final component in our paradigm. It addresses the need to be followers of Jesus in our reproducing. Coaches speak truth into our lives at key times and model for us what it means to be Jesus in the life of another person. Authentic disciples are also coaches for others in their journeys of discipleship.

Why is coaching so vital? Why is it an essential component in what constitutes authentic discipleship? For starters, coaching is biblical.

> *Brethren, join in following my example, and observe those who walk according to the pattern you have in us.*
> Philippians 3:17

> *The one who is taught the word is to share all good things with the one who teaches him.*
> Galatians 6:6

> *Just as you learned it from Epaphras, our beloved fellow bond-servant, who is a faithful servant of Christ on our behalf.*
> Colossians. 1:7

*Now if Timothy comes, see that he is with you without cause to be afraid, for he is doing the Lord's work, as I also am.*
1 Corinthians 16:10

*We proclaim Him, admonishing every man and teaching every man with all wisdom, that we may present every man complete in Christ.*
Colossians 1:28

Paul often demonstrated in his letters that discipleship is not done alone. It is a journey we take with others. "Careful investigation of Acts and Paul's writings shows that the apostle almost always had others with him on his missionary travels. On the rare occasions when he was alone, it is never long before he moves on to find one of his companions."[1]

The most effective way to impart knowledge is through life-on-life coaching. Paul followed Christ's model of discipleship by engaging men and women in "a come with me and learn" approach, rather than a "sit here and listen" model. The coaching process was a holistic and dynamic relationship. It was transformational, not transactional, for both the mentor and disciple alike. It was not the dissemination of facts and figures. Rather, it was intensive, reflective, and self-disclosing in nature.

Marvin R. Wilson explains the coaching component as given by the apostle Paul to Timothy, his protégé.

> The making of disciples results in the training of others to teach. Good teaching produces a chain reaction. The task Paul outlined to Timothy embraces four groups of teachers: 'And the things you have heard me say in the presence of many witnesses entrust to reliable men who will be qualified to teach others' (2 Tim. 2:2). This same Timothy from infancy knew the 'holy Scriptures,' that is the Old Testament (2 Tim. 3:15). Doubtless, Timothy's knowledge of the Scriptures in his early years and his 'sincere faith' that grew from this knowledge, came largely through the chain of godly family teachers to

> which he was linked: his grandmother Lois and mother Eunice (see 2 Tim, 1:5).[2]

Coaching allows for shared experiences and common real-life situations. It is not academic, cerebral, or passive. Rather, it is an active participation process in which the disciple learns from the mentor by observation, disciplined thinking, intensive contemplation, and application. The coach allows the disciple to try and to fail. A time of reflection and feedback occurs. The process is see one, do one, teach one.

> *The coaching model is couched in a relational framework that includes intensive accountability.*

The coaching model is couched in a relational framework that includes intensive accountability. It involves the disciple's identifying with the coach's perspective, as well as person. This mentoring process is not optional.

Coaching is about interdependence, which is nothing new. It is essentially Christian and it has been the pattern since the beginning of time.

A lot of foolishness can be avoided because of coaching relationships. Scripture says, "Without consultation, plans are frustrated, But with many counselors they succeed."[3]

God didn't intend for us to live in isolation. We've been created in the context of community through the sexual relationship of our mother and father, whether we grew up knowing them or not. Likewise, it's God's intention that we be raised in the context of a family, whether natural or adoptive.

Believers are baptized into the body of Christ, the church. Thus, we are members of His body. None of us has every spiritual gift, so we're dependent upon each other. Scripture paints a beautiful picture that there is no such thing as an independent disciple. Our identity is in relation to the other members of the body.

> *For even as the body is one and yet has many members, and all the members of the body, though they are many, are one*

*body, so also is Christ. For by one Spirit we were all baptized into one body, whether Jews or Greeks, whether slaves or free, and we were all made to drink of one Spirit. For the body is not one member, but many. If the foot should say, "Because I am not a hand, I am not a part of the body," it is not for this reason any the less a part of the body. And if the ear should say, "Because I am not an eye, I am not a part of the body," it is not for this reason any the less a part of the body. If the whole body were an eye, where would the hearing be? If the whole were hearing, where would the sense of smell be? But now God has placed the members, each one of them, in the body, just as He desired. If they were all one member, where would the body be? But now there are many members, but one body.*

*And the eye cannot say to the hand, "I have no need of you"; or again the head to the feet, "I have no need of you." On the contrary, it is much truer that the members of the body which seem to be weaker are necessary; and those members of the body which we deem less honorable, on these we bestow more abundant honor, and our less presentable members become much more presentable, whereas our presentable members have no need of it. But God has so composed the body, giving more abundant honor to that member which lacked, so that there may be no division in the body, but that the members may have the same care for one another. And if one member suffers, all the members suffer with it; if one member is honored, all the members rejoice with it. Now you are Christ's body, and individually members of it.*

1 Corinthians 12:12-27

One of my seminary professors suggested that it's impossible for people to be Christians if they're not part of a local church. A classmate was pretty upset and debated the professor. It turns out this student hadn't been part of a church in quite some time. The professor's logic centered on the fact that community has everything to do with our faith. It's how we live out the kingdom. It's how we do the many "one another" commands presented in the Bible. It's how we practice discipline and restoration. It's how the whole world will know that we're His disciples, by our love for each other. If we're not part of a local church, and we just love ourselves, it would be hard for the world to know that we are His disciples.

Cyprian, an early church father, sheds light on how the church viewed itself in regard to spiritual training, "No one can have God as Father who does not have the Church as Mother."[4] While some would debate the theological accuracy of this statement, one cannot ignore the ecclesiology represented in Cyprian's view. His statement is reflective of how his contemporaries viewed the early church. The church took its role of making disciples seriously. Eventually corruption did creep into this mind-set, but the church was convinced that making disciples was its responsibility. Another church father, Tertullian, had similar views. "If we think of catechesis in terms of the image of gestation before the spiritual birth, it comes as no small surprise that this gestation takes place within the nurturing context of the Church community, which early Christians referred to as their mother."[5]

"No one can have God as Father who does not have the Church as Mother."

## Avoidable Hypocrisy

Coaching relationships invite people to take off their masks and look into the mirror. The mirror is held by a group of caring people who are also in the journey. Robert Banks describes more about this journey.

> It is through the sharing of a person's life as well as their beliefs that life-giving change comes to others. Truth must be embodied as well as articulated, incarnated as well as revealed. Doing this sometimes drains the life out of the one who is sharing with others, but it is precisely this that brings the greatest life to them. It is, as Paul says, a case of "death in me, but life in you."[6]

Within such relationships we can share struggles and express genuine concern for others. Coaching relationships allow men and women to let down their guard and ask for help. It's a framework that promotes integrity. When we cut ourselves off from other believers, we set ourselves up to fail.

Coaching also invites authenticity. It gives permission for others, who have our best interest in mind, to ask questions about how we're doing in our marriages, friendships, thought life, devotional life, prayer life, and life itself. It allows concern without condemnation. There is nothing biblical about believers facing the battle alone. As we function within relationships that allow for accountability, we begin to understand the significant part we play in the life of another.

Coaching is the antithesis of hypocrisy. "On August 27, 1996, three weeks before his unexpected death, Henri Nouwen wrote: 'I am learning that the best cure for hypocrisy is community. Hypocrisy is not so much the result of not living what I preach but more of not confessing my inability to fully live up to my own words.'"[7]

*Coaching is the antithesis of hypocrisy.*

Everyone needs spiritual coaches. Coaching relationships give others permission to ask the tough questions. We all have a sin nature that seeks to dominate us. Coaches have the opportunity and privilege to peer deep into our thoughts (knowing), habits (being), and actions (doing). No one is a self-made man or woman. "No one lives or acts in isolation, and we are all affected by each other's behavior."[8] Scripture dogmatically claims that "Iron sharpens iron, so one man sharpens another."[9]

## The Age-Old Model

The Hebrew model of discipleship has always involved coaching relationships. "Coaching" may be a buzzword today, but it's a very ancient concept. Other terms like rabbi, mentor, spiritual director, master, and teacher have been used to describe such relationships.

Coaching relationships emerged, both positively and negatively, as early as the Garden of Eden. God coached Adam and Eve in the way of righteousness. Their relationship was authentic, honest, and transformational. However, almost as quickly, Satan offered his own type of coaching. His coaching centered on deceit, death, and destruction.

As the centuries passed, coaching continued to be a consistent theme in the Scriptures. Moses was perhaps the first leader to suffer from the "messiah complex." He thought he could do it all, and he wasn't only killing himself, but also those around him. God used a great coach to bring clarity to Moses' situation. Moses' coach was his father-in-law, Jethro.

> *Moses' father-in-law said to him, "The thing that you are doing is not good. You will surely wear out, both yourself and these people who are with you, for the task is too heavy for you; you cannot do it alone. Now listen to me: I will give you counsel, and God be with you. You be the people's representative before God, and you bring the disputes to God, then teach them the statutes and the laws, and make known to them the way in which they are to walk, and the work they are to do. Furthermore, you shall select out of all the people able men who fear God, men of truth, those who hate dishonest gain; and you shall place these over them as leaders of thousands, of hundreds, of fifties and of tens. Let them judge the people at all times; and let it be that every major dispute they will bring to you, but every minor dispute they themselves will judge. So it will be easier for you, and they will bear the burden with you. If you do this thing and God so commands you, then you will be able to endure, and all these people also will go to their place in peace." So Moses listened to his father-in-law and did all that he had said.*
>
> Exodus 18:17-24

Moses was able to transcend his problem because someone held a mirror up to his situation. Jethro had the courage and compassion to call Moses out regarding his poor leadership style. Moses had good intentions, but he was on the road to burnout.

Jethro's advice centered on our fourth measurement, reproducing. Jethro told Moses that if he wanted to push to the next level as a leader, he must reproduce himself in the lives of others. He couldn't continue to function at his current capacity unless he made more disciples.

Moses did just that. He reproduced himself in the lives of others according to Exodus 18:20. He taught them the statutes and laws (theology). He made them know the way in which they should walk (spiritual formation). He made them understand the work which they were to do (ministry). And the entire process was done through coaching relationships (reproducing). What was the result? Because Moses measured up as a disciple, he was also able to make other disciples.

It didn't stop there though. Just as Jethro coached Moses, Moses then coached Joshua. Robert Banks comments,

> Joshua was Moses' companion, and had been since his youth. As Moses' 'right hand,' he accompanied him where others, including the elders, did not. He was present when Moses received divine revelation for the people, and when Moses dealt with the people's response. Joshua was also the only one admitted to, and allowed to remain in, the tent set up outside the camp where God spoke directly to Moses.[10]

I hope you're beginning to see that our paradigm is not only accurate, but also interrelated. The whole of Scripture supports it. (See "Relevant Verses" at the end of this book.)

As the centuries wore on, coaching relationships continued, even in secular society. In the Greco-Roman model, philosophers like Socrates, Plato, and Aristotle took students fully upon themselves and trained them in a holistic approach. Within this framework, "Mastery of thought forms and exacting reproduction by memory drills were the emphases."[11] Rabbinic academies emerged where students lived in the homes of presiding rabbis. "The teacher was a possessor of knowledge and the pupil a blank slate, *tabula rasa*, to be written upon."[12]

Jesus utilized the relational coaching approach with His twelve disciples. While discipleship of the past often involved the potential for position and status, Jesus proposed a servant-leadership paradigm. Jesus' discipleship was counter-cultural. He had the disciples "*unlearn* their conventional modalities of leadership."[13] He endorsed discipleship that functioned within the context of real life. The Twelve did not learn theory or philosophy; they learned "in the way" as life happened. "Jesus is unlike other rabbis in that He does not emphasize memory drills, but a changed disposition in life, in all its habits."[14]

*Jesus' discipleship was counter-cultural. He had the disciples "unlearn their conventional modalities of leadership."*

Jesus gave ministry assignments to His disciples. At times, this included mundane responsibilities, such as distributing and gathering food.[15] These simple tasks revealed their level of faithfulness. Other times, these assignments involved being sent out, two by two, into nearby towns, to preach the kingdom of God and to heal the sick.[16] After returning from those ministry trips, the disciples shared their stories with Jesus. They had time for feedback with their mentor. This type of discipleship was built upon relational interaction, evaluation, and reflection.

## Different Strokes for Different Folks

Coaching relationships are a consistent theme throughout Scripture. Naomi coached Ruth. Elijah coached Elisha. Mordecai coached Esther. Nathan coached David. Eli coached Samuel, and in the end, Samuel coached Eli. There are too many coaches in the Bible to list here. Ironically, no two of these coaching relationships were alike. Some were very intense, almost a life-on-life apprenticeship. Others were a more situational or periodic interaction. Still, the underlying issue is that none of these people did it alone. All were interdependent.

Throughout history, disciples have also had many different types of coaching relationships. Some were less hierarchical.

Rather than a huge difference between master and apprentice, such relationships took on more of a partnership flavor. Although one person was clearly mentoring the other, they ministered alongside each other. Robert Banks "unpacks" this type of scenario:

> We should think of the relationship between these people as lying somewhere between a formal 'school' and an informal 'fellowship.' Some direct instruction took place. There was a communal dimension to their life, but the emphasis is mainly working together in common mission. It was as the younger heard the words, witnessed the action, and observed the life of the older that learning occurred, as well as the practical experience of working alongside them.[17]

Other coaching relationships were more intensive. Such is the case within the monastic system described by Jean Leclercq. "In general, monks did not acquire their religious formation in a school, under a scholastic, by means of the *quaestio,* but individually, under the guidance of an abbot, a spiritual father, through the reading of the Bible…within the liturgical framework of the monastic life."[18]

In such schools, disciples submitted to their spiritual fathers. Yet no human could ever replace the coaching of the Holy Spirit. The Holy Spirit is the true coach for every believer. Interestingly though, the Holy Spirit uses men and women to play a role in the coaching process. For followers of Jesus, I believe that such relationships are to be predominantly with the same gender in order to avoid sexual temptation. That isn't to say that men can never offer coaching to women or women to men. The Bible supports this model at times as well. Yet, coaching does involve intimacy, and therefore caution must be exercised. "Now a disciple, *mathētēs,* is a pupil, a learner, one who follows a religious teacher and is involved in an intimate fellowship and relationship with that teacher."[19]

Some coaching relationships almost resemble a live-in situation. Robert Banks explains this in *Reenvisioning Theological Education*.

> Teachers sat to instruct their students, with the latter at their feet. The teacher framed the questions, and there was regular repetition to drive a point home. The practice of physically "following" a teacher around demonstrated students' subservience, for they were to display the same fear and reverence to the teacher as they would to the Law he taught and embodied. Students were servants of their teacher (Aboth VI:5), fetching his sandals (T Neg 8,2), and performing other duties. They spent time in his home, accompanied him in his work, and went with him wherever he went. In this way the pupil not only listened to the teacher's words but also observed and imitated his actions. So learning was centered on a way of life rather than a set of lessons.[20]

Many religions in many different countries boast of extreme forms of coaching structures. These other religions don't have a corner on discipleship. I believe they borrowed their structures from the model Jesus gave us with His Twelve. *Understanding Christian Missions*, by J. Hebert Kane, showcases some of these situations.

> For the real meaning of disciple we must go to India, where the disciple chooses a particular guru and proceeds to attach himself to this person, living under his roof, sitting at his feet, eating at his table, listening to his words, walking and talking with him in the bazaar or the marketplace, even helping him with household chores. In a word, he shares the total life of the guru. In the give-and-take of this intimate fellowship the disciple gradually takes on the character of his guru. Before long he

> finds himself thinking, talking, acting like him. When he gets through he is a carbon copy of the guru. That is discipleship.[21]

All in all, whether coaching relationships are intensive or more casual in nature, they hold one thing in common. They "consist of people who have the integrity to come clean."[22] One might well argue that it's impossible for one to follow Jesus via spiritual formation, unless he or she is involved in coaching relationships. "Community is where real spiritual formation happens."[23]

## The Truth Doesn't Have to Hurt

Jean Vanier states, "Community is a place of pain, of death of ego."[24] In community, we are sacrificing independence and the pseudo-security of being unapproachable. We live this pain only if we are certain that for us being in community is our response to a call from God.[25] Like all relationships this side of heaven, coaching may hurt. Coaches are not perfect either and they may disappoint.

Just as our whole measurement paradigm acts as a mirror, so do coaching relationships. Unless we're truly committed to the discipleship process, therefore, we'll often flee at the first sight of pain. No one wants to have his weaknesses exposed. No one wants to see how she needs to improve. Our normal reaction is to cover up, to run away, to hide. Yet we must stay. We must pursue loving relationships. Coaching is not condemnation. It's truth framed and fueled by love.

Coaching is not condemnation. It's truth framed and fueled by love.

It takes a strong person to admit that he or she doesn't have it all together. Receiving godly coaching and applying the wisdom of that godly coaching takes humility. Rehoboam is an example of a person who received coaching, but rejected it. Rehoboam sought coaching from wise elders. He also sought coaching from his young friends. Each gave completely different advice.

Unfortunately, he listened to what he *wanted* to hear, rather than what he *needed* to hear. He listened to the coaching of his young friends. As a result, the kingdom of Israel split.

The path of discipleship isn't easy. On some levels, with a coach it's even more difficult. Yet in the end, a godly coach makes the whole journey a lot less painful. My advice is to get close to godly people around you. Ask some mature saints you know, the ones who are Christlike, to speak truth into your life. Consider what they say. Pray about it. Compare it with the Word. If it resonates with Scripture and the Holy Spirit's leading, follow their counsel. Then consider yourself richly blessed to have a loving coach, because they're few and far between. And don't forget that you must be a coach to others on their journeys of discipleship. Because, quite simply, you're probably farther along spiritually than some people you know, and they need what you can give them. They need to see Christ in you.

> When learners have been fully taught they will be like their teachers (cf. Lk. 6:40). Teachers not only teach the content of the syllabus, they teach attitudes and values. Students learn to emulate their teachers; in fact, they become like their teachers. Their resemblance is often described even in secular settings by saying, "He is that person's disciple," meaning, "He is like that person."
>
> Edgar J. Elliston and J. Timothy Kauffman

# The Component Paradigm

*You are searching for the magic key that will unlock the door to the source of power; and yet you have the key in your own hands.*

Napoleon Hill

Turn back to page 079 and look at the component paradigm again. Notice that, just as with our measurement paradigm, each specific component is inherently tied to every other component. Notice, also, for a stool to support weight, it must have four legs. Three legs will hold some weight, but it's not as stable as four. For disciples to be stable, they must integrate all four components into their daily lives. They must be followers of Jesus in their theology, spiritual formation, ministry, and coaching. If people allow only one component in their lives, then they often lean toward an extreme and fail to be authentic disciples.

Theology, spiritual formation, ministry, and coaching must be interconnected and integrated. We dare not allow a dualism to exist. The Bible warns that even if one knows all mysteries and all knowledge yet fails to have love in his or her being, then he or she is nothing.[1] Knowledge means little when divorced from being or doing.

God's people are called to "integrity of life in all its spiritual and social dimensions."[2] In our discussion of authentic discipleship we've examined the dangers of a compartmentalized life.

Throughout history when the church understood this danger and was careful to avoid it, it made great strides in its presence and witness. At times, pockets of people "got it." People, such as the Puritans, were committed to a unity of truth that touched all facets of life.[3]

The key is integrity in all of life. Forget compartments. Forget dualism. Dualism is permissible and welcomed within the Greek mind-set. "The Greek world did not understand education to be tied to the holiness of life. Rather, teaching primarily involved the transference of knowledge in the intellectual and technical areas."[4]

Yet this compartmentalization was not permitted within the Judeo-Christian tradition. "For the early Christians there was no fundamental distinction between learning (especially theological learning) and everyday life."[5] If we could fully understand what this means, the whole world would be changed. Andrew Kirk, in *Theology and the Third World Church Outreach and Identity*, paints a picture of the possibilities. He writes,

> [Such proponents] will become less like blotting paper which absorbs a stream of facts, than channels who take what they are receiving from tutors and allow it to fill the relevant cracks and crevices of the world they know. They will strive to appropriate the theology they study for themselves rather than just learn it as a series of facts. Its overriding purpose will be to form disciples of Jesus rather than to learn information about discipleship.[6]

Discipleship is possible only if and when we incorporate theology, spiritual formation, ministry, and coaching into our lives as we follow Jesus.

**As long as *theology* is seen as relevant only for *professional ministers*, the world will not be changed.**

"In the clerical paradigm, 'theology' is for ministers (the leadership of a faith community), not human beings, students, or laity."[7] The problem is not theology. The problem is the clerical paradigm. Jesus said the greatest commandment included loving God with our minds. God desires that we know Him. He desires *yada*. Robert Banks writes about *yada*:

> Although there is no static definition of the word *yada* in the Old Testament, it generally refers to knowledge—of God, others, and the world—that comes through experience. It springs from whole-hearted as well as whole-minded engagement with reality, leading to what we might call a whole-willed response. This stands in contrast to a detached, dispassionate, objective knowing that requires only a cognitive response.[8]

**As long as *spiritual formation* is seen as relevant only for *monks*, the world will not be changed.**

The Gnostic paradigm is the problem. Proponents "taught that by learning certain formulas and by submitting to certain rites, union with God and salvation could be attained without holiness of life."[9] True discipleship means that what we know is who we are, and who we are is what we know. "The study of theology is a process of spiritual formation."[10]

**As long as *ministry* is seen as relevant only for *faith-based charities*, the world will not be changed.**

The paradigm of a hermeneutic devoid of application is the problem. If we fail to apply truth, quite simply we have failed. "Our task is one of applying the ancient text in our modern context."[11] Who we are must be what we do, and what we do is essentially who we are. "Effective ministry emerges out of the quality of character—not out of technical competence. Maturity in ministry includes not only the technical abilities, the abilities to do the tasks at hand, but also the appropriately developed spiritual gifts which are employed through the fruit of the Spirit."[12]

**As long as *coaching* is seen as relevant only for *corporate executives*, the world will not be changed.**

The fact that the corporate world's paradigm has had the corner on coaching is the problem. Jesus modeled coaching. He taught His disciples *in* the way and *on* the way. His disciples had interactive experiences as they did ministry with their teacher. They heard the words, witnessed the action, and observed the life of their teacher. Christ coached them by giving them feedback. It was a holistic experience. By its very nature theology is best taught within the context of relationships. "Theology is education which provides knowledge not merely to be applied but first and foremost to be passed on—to be transmitted."[13]

## That Larger Story (Again)

If we become followers of Jesus in our knowing, being, doing, and reproducing, life as we know it will be different. The complete paradigm of discipleship, with its measurements and components, is not a new idea. It is the heart of God. It has been His plan since the beginning. He has always wanted a *called out* people, a transformed remnant who would embody the transformed life to the watching world. The display of transformation is for the sole purpose of drawing others into God's larger story, the story of the seed. Both Israel and Jesus reflect the prophetic call for everyone to be "a new person within the community of God's people on earth."[14] If Christianity becomes a changed life, if disciples become who they're born to be, the world will be forever changed.

# Part 4

# WHAT ARE YOU WAITING FOR?

# Living a Life Larger than Yourself

*Our deepest fear is not that we are inadequate. Our deepest fear is that we are powerful beyond measure. It is our own light, not our darkness, that most frightens us. We ask ourselves, who am I to be brilliant, gorgeous, talented and fabulous? Actually, who are you not to be? You are a child of God. Your playing small doesn't serve the world. There's nothing enlightened about shrinking so that other people won't feel insecure around you. We were born to manifest the glory of God that is within us. It's not just in some of us, it's in everyone. And as we let our light shine, we unconsciously give other people permission to do the same. As we are liberated from our own fear, our presence automatically liberates others.*

Nelson Mandela quoting Marianne Williamson

There's a secret club out there. I guess it has always existed; I just didn't find out about it until our little boy, Keegan, was born. Prior to his birth, parents I met would give me the initiation wink. I never picked up on it. However, one day I finally got it. Now when parents wink at me, I wink back. I'm part of the secret club.

You see, parents know something that people without kids don't know. I'm not joking. I'm dead serious. Before Keegan was born, I used to do this thing called sleep. Eight hours of sleep seems like a foreign experience now. Instead, now I just exist. There is no day. There is no night. Life just kind of is. Sometimes I'm awake and I don't know it. Other times I'm asleep and I don't know it. Sometimes when I wake up in the morning I realize that I fed Keegan three times the night before. I don't consciously remember, but the three bottles in the sink bear some sort of proof.

In the middle of the night during feedings, there is not much to do. Those times when I'm awake, I sometimes watch poker. I never knew how interesting poker can be at 2:30 in the morning. I didn't grow up playing it. Now I know all about poker and the people who play it professionally. Keegan and I watch poker together. Sometimes I read my Bible when I feed him at 2:30 a.m. Other times I pray. But sometimes I'm exhausted so I just watch good old poker.

It takes a while to learn all the terms of poker. One of the most popular poker games is Texas Hold 'Em. While watching this game, I learned what phrases like "The Flop," "The Turn," and "The River" mean. What makes Texas Hold 'Em so exciting is the "all in" move. When someone goes "all in" they basically bet all their chips on the hand they're holding. It's a gutsy move and there is no turning back. It's "all or nothing." It's "do or die."

In the poker shows, a lot of players start out at the table. Slowly, one by one, different ones are knocked out. When only two players are left, it's called head to head action. This is when the game gets exciting. The player with the most chips is called the chip leader. If the chip leader has a good hand, he'll put enough chips into the pot to force his opponent to make an extremely tough decision. Usually when this happens the tension grows thick. The crowd hushes and hangs on the edge of their seats. The player who is left has one of two choices. He can go "all in" or he can fold. If he wants to commit, he'll put in all of his chips, going "all in." If he wants to walk away from the hand, he'll fold.

Maybe it's an odd thought, but I think following Jesus is like poker. Christ invites you to go head to head with Him. As the Son of God, He is *the* chip leader. He put all His chips on you and forces you to make a decision. At this point the tension grows. The world hangs on the edge of its seat. You have one of two choices. You can either commit and go "all in" or you can fold. It's your call.

## Going All In

That is what this book is all about. It's about going "all in." I don't see Christ giving any other option. He's called you. It's your move. He's said, "Follow Me." Will you or won't you? It's that simple. You'll either holistically follow Jesus in your knowing, being, doing, and reproducing, or you won't follow Him at all. You can't go halfway.

That is not to say that you or I will ever be perfect. Authentic discipleship doesn't mean that we won't fail or falter. We will. It's inevitable, but Jesus can handle that. What He won't handle is a life of pseudo-allegiance.

> *Authentic discipleship doesn't mean that we won't fail or falter. We will.*

Often we think of authentic disciples as super saints. The reality is we're all on a journey. Some of us are baby Christians. This isn't a bad thing if we've recently begun our journey following Jesus. But it's a bad thing if we've been at that stage for years.

When Keegan was born, he couldn't do much at all. I didn't question whether he was alive or not. I didn't doubt he was real. He let my wife Kelly and me know. He cried. He urinated. He ate. And he slept. Really that's about all he did. Weeks went by before he gave us a true smile. Then he got a little older. Later he even rolled over. Almost every day he did something more than he did the day before. He failed at times. He tried to hold his head up and then he got tired. His head fell down quickly. Other times he tried to crawl. Sometimes he only slid his nose across the blanket. He became frustrated and cried.

The point is, he was trying. He was growing. He was progressing. He was learning new things. Keegan was alive. We never doubted that.

When we went to our pediatrician, he asked questions about Keegan. He asked us if he was gaining weight and lifting his head. He charted Keegan's height. He didn't ask if Keegan could walk or ride a bike or read at that time. Obviously, he was not supposed to yet. He was only a baby.

The same is true of Christians. If we're new believers, we're not supposed to be at the same place as a ten-year-old Christian. The question is not whether we are at a certain level yet. The real question is "Are we growing?" Are we progressing? It's okay that we fail as long as we're trying. We're supposed to be only a little bit different than the day before. We'll get discouraged pretty fast if we start comparing ourselves to everyone else around. That's not the point.

This book is like a mirror. It is meant to show us the true bar of discipleship that Jesus presented. It's meant to demonstrate that Jesus doesn't separate followers into two different classes: those who sort of follow Him and those who truly follow Him. Jesus doesn't lower the bar for us. He gives us the power to reach it, but He certainly doesn't lower it.

Jesus didn't invite us to be part of a cool little club. He didn't ask us to make a one-time decision, or even attend church. Jesus "did not invite people to adopt a certain philosophy, or even join a certain group, but to come to a relationship with him."[1] Discipleship is a holistic relationship. It is following Jesus with our knowing, being, doing, and reproducing. It's pursuing Him with our head, heart, and hands. Discipleship is integrating theology, spiritual formation, ministry, and coaching into our lives.

It's using this life to prepare for the next one. It's losing our life to truly find it. Discipleship is giving away what we can't keep to gain what can never be taken away. It's inviting death of self while traveling the path of life. It's releasing what isn't ours to hold and holding the One who will never let us go. It's dying when we're still alive, so that we may live when it's our time to die.

## Making Mud Pies

Most of us give up too easily. We have a burning desire deep inside. We know that we've been called to a great adventure.

We feel the ache, but we have tried to bury it with busyness, achievements, and relationships. Yet at strange, unpredictable times, it emerges. In peculiar moments, when heaven and earth seem to kiss, it lashes out violently, seeking to embrace us.

We sense it when we taste the beauty in the world. We feel it when the warm breeze blows on our face while we walk beside the ocean. We see it when shadows lengthen, and the moon presents its pale face in the distance. We know it when we walk in the fall and see colored leaves dance across our path. Creation is God's subtle invitation for us to join Him in the journey. He's all around, wooing us. He's inviting us to a grand adventure that exceeds any thought we could ever think.

> *Creation is God's subtle invitation for us to join Him in the journey.*

We have a choice. God wants us to be part of His story. He wants us to abandon our small stories and join the larger story that He's been writing since before time began. But so often we can't see it. Certainly we can't control it. Most of us would rather live, trying to ignore the ache we feel inside because we have not pursued His larger story. We would rather silence the deep desire that would propel us to Him if only we would embrace it.

In *Mere Christianity* C. S. Lewis unpackaged the essence of these "small stories" that we often die chasing. "We are half-hearted creatures fooling about with drink and sex and ambition when infinite joy is offered us, like an ignorant child who wants to go on making mud pies in the slums because he cannot imagine what is meant by the offer of a holiday at the sea. We are far too easily pleased."[2]

## One Disciple's Legacy

Perhaps you know about one of the saddest stories I've ever heard. On the morning of October 30, 2005, the 33 year-old pastor of the University Baptist Church in Waco, Texas, was electrocuted in the middle of a baptismal service. Pastor Kyle Lake "was standing in water up to his shoulder. He was grabbing the microphone so everyone could hear" when suddenly, he was electrocuted.[3] He died shortly after, leaving a wife and three young children.

> He was grabbing the microphone so everyone could hear when suddenly, he was electrocuted.

I'm told that Kyle Lake was a faithful disciple. The morning of his death, he was going to preach through Jeremiah 29, using the movie *Garden State* as a backdrop. Both refer to a homesickness of sorts. I received a copy of his sermon notes from that morning. It's a sermon he never got to preach. Yet it's one that I'm told he lived. His message cuts in below with a quote from Melody Porter, his concluding thoughts about *Garden State*, and then strangely, his last words about living fully in this life.

> Melody Porter says, "The problem with that future focus is that we miss God's presence, God's unexpected presence in the here and now…as Henri Nouwen says, 'the treasure you are looking for is hidden in the ground on which you stand.' It's so much easier to think that the answer is in the future, because that takes some of the pressure off what we're supposed to be doing in the here and now. It also helps us to deny whatever pain is in the here and now, and look instead to a time when our lives will REALLY begin, when things will be different. But God is right here, right now...in whatever foreign landscape that lacks meaning, in whatever foreign landscape that leaves us unsettled. God is constantly creating new possibilities in this life, even in the places that we yearn to run from."
>
> Conclusion of *Garden State*: At the end of the movie, Largeman has undergone this transformation. For the first time in his life, he's realized this sense of homesickness that he's felt for so many years—that he's been running from that he's prevented himself

from feeling. But what Sam does is that she gives him permission to be himself. To EXPERIENCE the here and now. In a relationship of honesty and vulnerability. In grieving the death of his mom. In the comfort, warmth and messiness of friendship.

And here I think God is saying to each of us, "Abandon your plans of escape. And be where you are. Plant gardens and live and live well." I don't know what your planting gardens may look like but let me end there by trying to provide a glimpse into what that may be like:

Live. And Live Well. BREATHE. Breathe in and Breathe deeply. Be PRESENT. Do not be past. Do not be future. Be now. On a crystal clear, breezy 70 degree day, roll down the windows and FEEL the wind against your skin. Feel the warmth of the sun.

If you run, then allow those first few breaths on a cool Autumn day to FREEZE your lungs and do not just be alarmed, be ALIVE. Get knee-deep in a novel and LOSE track of time.

If you bike, pedal HARD…and if you crash then crash well. Feel the SATISFACTION of a job well done—a paper well-written, a project thoroughly completed, a play well-performed. If you must wipe the snot from your 3-year old's nose, don't be disgusted if the Kleenex didn't catch it all…because soon he'll be wiping his own.

If you've recently experienced loss, then GRIEVE. And grieve well. At the table with friends and family, LAUGH. If you're eating and laughing at the same time, then might as well laugh until you puke. And if you eat, then SMELL. The aromas are not impediments to your day. Steak on the grill, coffee beans freshly ground, cookies in the oven.

And TASTE. Taste every ounce of flavor. Taste every ounce of friendship. Taste every ounce of Life. Because-it-is-most-definitely-a-Gift.[4]

## It's Your Choice

Discipleship is embracing our homesickness. It is giving up a lifestyle of anesthetizing the pain; it's embracing the ache. It's feeling it fully so that it drives you to Jesus even more. It's throwing your coping mechanisms in the trash and for the first time truly living. It's a vibrant and authentic relationship with the only One who gives you permission to be your true self. He wants to be with you fully in the moment. God actually initiates this messy relationship called discipleship. God disrupts your small story on earth so that you can be part of His larger story in heaven. My challenge for you is to follow Jesus holistically.

*God disrupts your small story on earth so that you can be part of His larger story in heaven.*

Strangely, we're back where we started. The choice is yours to make. And it's your call because you've been called—called to become who you were *truly* born to be.

> If I find in myself a desire which no experience in this world can satisfy, the most probable explanation is that I was made for another world.
>
> C. S. Lewis

# Afterword

*We must get beyond textbooks,*
*go out into the by-paths and untrodden*
*depths of the wilderness and travel and explore*
*and tell the world the glories of our journey.*
John Hope Franklin

Thank you for your time, your trust, and your open-mindedness to read about a subject as profound as discipleship. In a way, this paradigm was an experiment. As you already know from the acknowledgments, the introduction, and probably now from reading the entire book, this project was born out of the frustration I felt when someone I knew got "saved." I didn't know what to do. I didn't have a paradigm to help me know where to start or how to measure legitimate progress.

That frustration turned into a paradigm. The paradigm began to take shape as I studied in my doctoral program. I worked it out in the halls of academia. I explored current and emerging trends within theological education and ecclesiology. But, to be honest, I knew that few people would sit down to read a dissertation titled, *A Model for Leadership Training through the Partnership of Grace Brethren Churches in the North Central Ohio District and Grace Theological Seminary*.

As a result, I began simultaneously to write this manuscript. I thought that other followers of Jesus were just as frustrated and confused as I was. I thought that our postmodern world was craving for an understandable, biblically trustworthy, and culturally relevant way of understanding discipleship. I had sat with enough people (teens, young adults, and older adults) who gave up because their Christianity wasn't working. It wasn't big enough.

The problem was not that Christianity wasn't cutting it. The problem was that *their* Christianity wasn't cutting it. It was too small. It was too impoverished. After all, the gospel isn't just accepting Jesus into one's heart; it's also following Him with your life. But what does *following* entail?

The project was to find out how "deep the rabbit hole goes." I hope you have realized that it is deep. Simple but deep. Jesus calls us to an adventure of epic proportions.

So what is the power of a paradigm? In and of itself, it's not worth much. Once incarnated, however, fireworks can begin to happen. Thus, while writing my dissertation and this manuscript, God began to put some pieces together.

Bono (*Time Magazine's* 2005 Person of the Year) has referred to the power of an idea. The new idea was taking shape in many different ways. The pastors and people at the Grace Brethren Church of Powell began to dream. Thus, Grace Institute began to take shape, and the people of the East Side Grace Brethren Church began to dream with us as well.

This Afterword is an account of the incarnation of the paradigm presented in this book. It is *Called* in real time with real people as demonstrated in Grace Institute. My website (KaryOberbrunner.com) contains a pictorial journey as well, in addition to frequent updates and significant outcomes (GI graduation, for example).

Feel free to use the thoughts, stories, or suggestions offered. Learn from my mistakes. This thing called discipleship is a group effort. If any of this resonates with you, drop me an e-mail (kary@karyobrunner.com). I'd love to hear what is happening in your experience. Chances are that wherever God takes my wife Kelly and me in life, we'll be working out this thing called discipleship because it's on His heart and it's His story.

— Kary Oberbrunner

What is Grace Institute? Simply, it is the embodiment of *Called*. It's the measurements and components lived out by real people in real settings. The remainder of this Afterword is divided into three sections 1) The Plan, 2) The Process, and 3) The People.

## The Plan

**Who we are:** Grace Institute is a model for leadership development that produces a community of life-long learners and laborers.

**Our Logo:**

**Our Vision:** (What we are trying to accomplish. Where we are going.)

To equip and empower current and emerging leaders to grow as authentic followers of Jesus Christ.

**Our Mission:** (How we plan to accomplish the vision. How we are going to get there.)

To partner with individuals and ministries to provide teaching, training, coaching, and consultation.

**The Measurements:**

The Bible provides checks and balances so we can confidently see how we measure up as authentic followers of Jesus.

1. **Knowing**—because following Jesus requires a cognitive choice based upon biblical truth. As followers, we are commanded to love God with our minds and pursue life-long learning.
2. **Being**—because following Jesus means we are to become more like Him every day. As followers, what we know must become who we are.
3. **Doing**—because following Jesus means He must be incarnated into our everyday lives. As followers, what we believe and who we are is revealed by what we do.

4. **Reproducing**—because following Jesus means we are bringing others with us on our journey. As followers, we are intentional about embodying Christ in our own lives and forming Him in others.

**The Components.** Although there are many methods of discipleship, the Bible provides us with four irreducible components essential to growing as authentic followers of Jesus.

1. **Theology**—because the Bible doesn't relegate the responsibility of theology to a professional vocation. Every follower is a theologian in thought and life and ministers from a deep reservoir of theology.
2. **Spiritual Formation**—because the Bible says being spiritually formed takes time and effort. Every follower must remain on a continuous journey toward Christ-likeness.
3. **Ministry**—because the Bible gives us the privilege of loving and serving others in practical ways. Every follower is a minister entrusted with spiritual gifts regardless of age, life-stage, gender, or vocation.
4. **Coaching**—because the Bible tells us we need others to help us in our journey. Every follower also needs to be coaching others who are not as far along in their journey.

## The Process

Grace Institute has many different expressions and tracks within the local church. These tracks and expressions range from seminars and electives to a full Continuing Education Certificate in Biblical Studies issued jointly from Grace Institute and Grace Theological Seminary (www.gts.grace.edu). One of our first Grace Institute efforts consisted of a summer leadership track. Twenty-two students, ranging from ages 12 to 24, committed to Grace Institute for the summer of 2006.

Our Requirements of the participants:

1. To spend an average of two days a week (Wednesdays and Fridays) in training (theological training and ministry field experience—roughly 20 hours a week).

2. To mentor a middle school student (included in the 20 hours).
3. To be mentored by a pastor or ministry leader (included in the 20 hours).
4. To help oversee a home-based Bible study (included in the 20 hours).
5. To treat these requirements with the same seriousness as a job.

**Our Commitment to the Participants:**

1. To equip, train, and empower students in theology, spiritual formation, and ministry skills.
2. To provide practical ministry experience couched in a framework of mentoring relationships.
3. To provide an opportunity for students to evaluate seriously God's call upon their lives regarding future full-time vocational ministry.
4. To allow others to validate a call in the students' lives for future ministry.
5. To make theoretical class work take on new meaning as the students encounter real people with real problems while living out real ministry.

## The People

To determine the success of Grace Institute, we asked the students to evaluate their experience. Here are evaluations from 11 of the 22 Grace Institute summer leadership students. Their comments are unedited. They are honest. They represent their reflections on the measurements, components, and the overall experience.

1. The expectations placed on my generation seem almost overwhelming at times. By the age of 18, students must come face to face with some of the most difficult and life-altering decisions of their lives.
   - Where do I go to college?
   - What do I study?
   - Where do I want to live?
   - How am I possibly going to pay for all of this?

The list goes on. Not only are these questions difficult enough, but it seems that this generation is in a frantic race to find the perfect answer. Isn't it ok to slow down and apply knowledge through genuine, authentic life experiences? Grace Institute allowed me to not only continue a formal education, but to also learn by Being, Doing, and Reproducing. After all, Knowing the information is not even half the battle.

**Being** active through prayer, worship, time with God, writing, and other activities is helpful because it creates an opportunity to grow personally.

**Doing** ministry together is useful because it allows students the chance to actually apply things that have been learned.

**Reproducing** through mentoring and coaching gives both the teacher and student room to grow by simply living life together.

Knowing without Being, Knowing without Doing, and Knowing without Reproducing is almost useless. Through the Grace Institute, I finally got the opportunity to not only learn new material, but to also genuinely apply it on a day-to-day basis.

– Ryan, Young Adult, Future Youth Pastor

2. To be honest I am really not sure how to start this. So much has happened this summer. One thing I know for sure is that this summer was unlike anything I have ever experienced. We started out the summer at Urban Concern. To me it was a good way to start, because I enjoy serving. It didn't stretch me very much though.

   I've grown up in a Christian family, and I've changed churches many times. It wasn't until GBC Powell that I really began my walk with God.

I accepted Christ at the "Superbowl" in middle school. There wasn't anybody I could really talk to there so I rededicated my life one night at youth group. Just last January I was baptized and now I've just finished Grace Institute. I used to think Christianity was just going to church and following the Ten Commandments. Now I know it's so much more.

I normally enjoy the serving part the most, but this summer was different. It was the theology part that I was excited for. Attending a public school, I don't exactly spend time reading and studying the Bible. The only time I really opened it was Sunday mornings and devotionals. But even then I don't go very deep.

On the second day of GI we went though Romans 1 verse by verse and I don't think I have ever enjoyed studying the Bible so much. Hermeneutics had a whole new meaning. The spiritual formation part was more relevant than ever. My view about life and where I am headed changed because of this summer. I am now considering full-time ministry. I am more open with my friends about God than ever and I feel more equipped to defend my faith.

I have always enjoyed ministry and serving others for God. It gives me such joy to see how thankful others are especially when usually what we're doing isn't difficult at all. I think God gave us a lot of energy to serve others and share our excitement.

Coaching (reproducing) touched me the most. I loved watching the middle school students step out and step up. They were willing to serve, lead, and teach. It was a blessing to watch them in Life Transformation Groups (LTGs) on Thursdays. I saw them get stretched through teaching their peers. I wish I had more time with them and with my coach.

– Beth, Liberty High School

3. Before Grace Institute I focused just on knowing the Bible and being a Christian. This summer has made me realize I need to be more involved in ministry. At first I was uncomfortable about leaving my "circle of safety," but once you meet the people and see their need for God you open up. I really enjoyed getting to share Christ's love through my ministry experiences. One of the things I learned through the Grace Institute and have begun to do with my friends is coaching them in their spiritual walks. We as Christians are called to spread the gospel as well as mentor those baby Christians in their new faith just like Paul mentored Barnabas. Without someone to guide them along the way, new Christians often lose faith and return to their old lifestyle. This is why having a mentor and accountability partner is so important to building a strong and steadfast walk.

   – Erinn, Worthington Christian Middle School

4. The four components of Grace Institute never really seemed relevant to me until the summer was coming to a close. Knowing, Being, Doing, and Reproducing were words that I assumed I should memorize because they were constantly included in our theology days and even in a game that Pastor Kary had us do to get us thinking about the four pillars of the Institute. Unfortunately, for me, I did not take time to reflect on what they would do to my daily ministry during Grace Institute. I would have been much more fruitful this summer had I taken the time to let these four words really sink in.

To me, the four pillars of Grace Institute are all about the personal desire that until recently I evidently lacked. On Wednesday I read John 17:21 which reads, "My prayer for all of them is that they will be one, just as you and I are one, Father—that just as you are in me and I am in you, so they will be in us, and the world will know that you sent me" (New Living Testament).

Because Christ is in me and I in Him, I do have that desire to know, be, do, and reproduce as Christ did while He walked the earth. That was His passion therefore should be anyone's who wants to be a true leader and follower of Christ. As a senior I've realized that I feel a sense of urgency about how I am perceived. I have one more year to prove that I am Christian. Sadly, yes that was what I thought it was all about. By participating in GI, I see that being a Christian and wanting people to recognize me instead of Christ is not why I was put on this earth and chosen by God. Just fulfilling one pillar (being) does not mean that I've done all I can in Christ. He wants me to add three more links to the "chain" of life. GI therefore, has taught me how to live because I am one with Christ. I need all four to be like Him and produce fruit that is pleasing to the Lord.

I think the component that I lacked the most before this summer was reproducing.

Ironically that is the pillar I had the desire to work on the most. Teaching the middle school Bible study forced me to coach many students at one time. Last night we finished the book of James and just had an awesome night of prayer, worship and confession. I was so encouraged when I asked someone if they would close us in prayer and a young man prayed about how thankful he was to have the Bible study and that he felt closer to God. I completely saw God work last night and realized that He was forming me into the leader and follower that He wants me to be for Him, one who uses knowing, being, doing, and reproducing to glorify God and fulfill His call on my life!

– Alyssa, Worthington Kilbourne High School

5. This summer at Grace Institute I learned and grew the most in my life on how to truly love God. The first thing I want to share that really helped me is that I learned how to talk to people about God, and how to start a conversation with them. Before this, that was one of my weakest areas and I was always nervous about talking to other people. I have already used this skill a little bit, and it will greatly help me in the future. Another thinking that I realized is to have a servant's heart. During the first ministry days, I just did things because someone told me to or I saw it had to be done. But I realized that I need to want to do it, and be willing to serve others.

   During the summer my communication with God really grew. I have started to pray about a lot of things. I want to grow even more and be praying constantly. I have also learned different ways to read my Bible, and things I should look for to understand it better. One last thing I want to say is that I have grown in becoming both a better leader and speaker. This has taught me what kinds of things I should say, and how I should talk to people. Co-leading the LTG was a great experience in becoming a better teacher.

   I would like to thank all of you who helped me grow in my faith and in my Christian life.

This has been a great experience I hope to continue in the future.

– Blake, Liberty High School

6. During the time at Grace Institute, I have learned and have been strengthened a lot. Through ministry days and theology days I learned how to be a better believer. The fellowship with other Christians impacted me. I decided to be a part of the Grace Institute because I wanted to grow and serve the Lord, but didn't have the opportunity until GI came along. I have now learned to know, be, do, and reproduce.

    I have been really struggling with letting go and letting God have ultimate control in my life. One day at GI we were all in a group talking about our faith and the struggles we were all facing. I realized that we all have struggles no matter what, but when you entrust God to take over your life you can handle anything. That really made an impression on me.

    I felt like I got a lot more out of ministry days this summer. Two of my favorites days were Urban Concern and Urban NBC. These two outreaches were both in the urban neighborhoods of Columbus. I was and still am surprised that these would be my favorite. The setting was just a big surprise to me. I also think what really touched my heart and my life was the hope in the kids' eyes. They didn't have everything we have, but they also relied more on Christ for everything.

    Grace Institute really opened my eyes to new things and God really placed His hand on my heart when things got tough. GI was a "wow" experience and there are really no words to describe what I felt and got to be a part of this summer.

– Brittany, Liberty High School

7. While at the mall I became discouraged because I didn't talk to anyone. I felt that I wasn't made to evangelize. Later on in GI from Mark's teaching about evangelism I learned that I was being selfish and putting myself and how I felt at that time above witnessing to people. I was pretty much condemning them to hell. I could be the person that God was going to use to save them but I became selfish and thought of myself instead. I fell short with applying those things in my life which hindered me from reproducing new Christians. Now when I am given the opportunity to talk to someone I strive to put my selfish ways behind me and to reach out to those people who are in need. There are still times when my selfish nature comes through and I lose sight of why I am here on this earth, what my mission is, but I pray to God to give me boldness and confidence to do what needs to be done and save the people who surround me every day.

   - Jacob, Worthington Christian High School

8. I've been sitting on a chair with only two legs for a while. "Knowing and Being" with an occasional "Doing" have been the legs of my chair. The idea of having four legs to my chair didn't even cross my mind. I thought I had it good with my two-legged chair, but now I see that I have been crippled in my walk as a Christian and wasn't expecting great things God has for me. When I see the four pillars it makes me think of how I love God with all my mind, heart and soul.

   Without the four pillars in my life, how can I be a Christian? How can I be a Christ- follower, if I don't follow the example Christ laid out for me? He did all four in a holistic fashion, not separating one from the other. I've been trying so hard to be balanced with my two-legged chair, but wouldn't four legs be better? I've been trying so hard to run my race with only the "knowing" and "being," without knowledge that there was more. Realizing this is a big step for me and maybe only now it is just starting to sink in. If I want to live a fulfilling life then I must do as Jesus did, through these tools of discipline. I have grown so much by incorporating these pillars in my life. I realize more and more that Christianity is not a suit that I wear, but a lifestyle that I live.

I have felt empty without all four pillars and I am starting to see the refreshing purpose of living all four pillars. There is so much more than being a Christian man filled with love compassion and gentleness. God has given us a spirit of power which we use for Him (2 Timothy 1:7). Instead of being the domesticated Christian man with no commitment to Jesus, I am to be a person that is constantly training and encouraging others, doing ministry, and worshiping God with my life. I simply love God first and then love people. This is the opposite of the "get out of jail free card" view of salvation.

– Abram, Delaware Hayes High School

9. This summer I had the opportunity to be a part of Grace Institute. I decided to take this challenge because I really wanted to become closer to God through theology, spiritual formation, ministry and coaching. Now, I would tell you what my favorite part of GI was but I can't pick just one thing. The theology part of GI was really sweet because I honestly knew hardly anything about the Bible. I go to a public school and I don't have the chance to take a Bible class. I definitely don't have a chance to really study the Bible. I also really enjoyed the spiritual formation part

of GI. There were days we would spend one hour with God where we could just pray and read our Bibles. Now at first it was kind of hard for me to focus during that time. I would just sit there and think. GI showed me different things that I could do during that time. I could write in my journal or write names of people I could pray for.

Another thing I enjoyed was the ministry days. We would go to places like the Short North to help with Urban NBC. I really enjoyed Urban NBC because we got to work with kids and I really love kids! Lastly, we coached middle school students while we were being coached as well. I feel like I learned a lot and that I will be able to pass that down to middle school students. I really loved GI and I really look forward to using the things I learned this summer. This experience definitely brought me closer to God.

– Ashley, Worthington Kilbourne High School

10. Here at the Grace Institute we learned four basic essentials that we would need in order to have a more powerful walk with the Lord Jesus. The four basic essentials consist of theology, spiritual formation, ministry, and coaching. These four categories were made in order to prepare the students in becoming powerful tools in God's work. I myself have found these components as being very helpful and also necessary in becoming a true leader. Being a leader in God's ministry is exactly what I want, so these components fit in well.

    By using theology I can be on the defense or offense when facing enemies of the faith. Having the knowledge of the Bible allows me to have a weapon in God's army. Without my theology I would be left with nothing to protect my faith. Spiritual formation is a process you go through that transforms you into a more powerful Christian. By worshiping and praying you find yourself closer to God. Ministry and serving allow one to be stretched from their comfort and overcome fear. I use ministry to set an example and to plant seeds. These basic essentials are so important because it is how others become followers of Christ.

The last component is coaching. This allows you to pass on your knowledge and experiences to others and in doing so you pass down the line of mentors. We are the paintbrushes in God's beautiful painting and in order to become a good reliable paintbrush you must obtain theology, perform spiritual formation, lead in ministry, and reproduce in coaching. By doing this, God's painting will look beautiful with your help.

– Cody, Worthington Christian High School

11. Grace Institute was the best thing for me this summer. It embodies the way a Christian is supposed to live, the way the church ought to be run, opportunities for fellowship, application of knowledge, theology, development of skills, and discipleship. The way a Christian should live is according to the way Jesus lived. In Luke 2:41-52 Jesus is 12 years old, yet intelligently discussing Scripture with Jewish teachers. Jesus shows His spiritual formation through all of the times He went alone to pray (Luke 22:39-44; Matthew 4:1-11). He knew Scripture as well. His ministry was phenomenal; and His coaching even more so. Jesus says to be like Him and to take His yoke upon us. So many times Christians don't do that. Grace Institute introduced to me, probably for the first time, the best way to be a Christian.

The only way to be a Christian is to follow the way of Jesus. In addition to this I learned that the church is a body of people following Jesus' way, not a building but a fellowship. I think I knew this before but it became more real to me through GI when we saw all different kinds of churches. The fellowship, discipleship, and opportunities offered throughout this summer have encouraged me beyond belief. Two of my new friends from GI told me that they can see me working with teenagers and I had never considered that area of ministry before. Now I think the idea appeals to me more and more.
– Stephanie, Worthington Christian High School

# Appendix: Uncovering a Seed Hermeneutic

Nothing is worse than showing up at a movie 10 minutes late. I don't mean just missing the previews. After all, people do that intentionally. I am talking about wanting to get to a movie on time, but somehow being delayed and missing part of the main feature. As a result, you enter a dark theater. Your eyes cannot see a thing. You are not accustomed to the new surroundings and it is difficult to perceive things clearly. As time passes, you eventually make out some shapes and spot an open seat in the back. As you climb over several people, finally and thankfully you slump down into your seat.

As you begin to watch the movie, you realize that because 10 minutes have already elapsed, you have no concept of the plot. You missed the opening scene and you are not quite sure who is the villain or who is the good guy. Without any concept of the struggle or larger story, you feel lost. Everything seems random and detached and you feel as though you have to add personal interpretation in order to fill in some of the blanks.

Sometimes we have the same experience when we read the Bible. Our hermeneutic (method of biblical interpretation) seems indistinct. We wander around through the text trying to make out the shapes. We are not accustomed to the surroundings and thus it is tough to have an accurate view of reality.

After some time, however, we begin to make sense of the environment. We take a seat and begin to consume the text. Unfortunately, it seems as if we have shown up to the text 10 minutes into the story. It is tough to get the full picture. Events seem unrelated.

Thankfully, when considering the text in regard to discipleship, we do not have to fill in the blanks. Rather, we will see that God has filled them in for us. Just as movie DVDs often provide a special disc with the director's commentary, it is as if we have the Author's commentary of the Bible available to us. He does not leave us to our own conclusions. "What distinguishes Scripture from all other books is that God Himself is the author. Other books speak to me about God, but in the Scripture it is God who speaks to me."[1]

How foolish it would be for us to take the Director's commentary and exchange it for the audience's. Sadly that is what we do many times. "The trend within contemporary hermeneutics is to allow the community to interpret the text."[2] Truth is not inherent to us individually or to our community. Rather, truth is a person who longs to interact with each of us through the text (John 14:6).

Of course we all read the text in different ways. After all, each one of us is created uniquely. "People perceive and experience God in different ways. What supports and encourages one person in their spiritual journey may have no effect whatsoever upon someone else."[3] In spite of this, however, we do not change the text in order to fit us. Rather, it is we who change as we read the text.

Another temptation when reading the Word is to take on the role of a critic. People sometimes attend movies with the purpose of critiquing them. In other words, they watch a movie with the goal of dissecting it. As a result, they fail to get caught up in the story. They watch it for the special effects or the breath-taking landscape. They remain distant and uninvolved.

When we read the Scriptures we can easily fall into the same trap. In such situations we find ourselves reading the Bible for its literary flair or how it will preach. We read it for information and not for transformation. As a result, we are in a position of power and remain uninvolved in the story. "Informational reading seeks to master the text. We seek to grasp it, to get our minds around it. We bring it under our control (interpretation) and defend it against any other controls (interpretations), so we can use the information to impose our agenda on the world."[4]

## The Story of the Seed

When we do read the Word correctly, when we listen to the Author's commentary and position ourselves in a place of openness, an interesting reality emerges. Regardless of where we enter the text, whether in the Law, the Psalms, the Prophets, the Gospels, or the Epistles, we see a consistent plot. We do not have to guess about the story line. The Creator has always intended for His godly seed to be spread throughout the earth. Beginning in Genesis and ending in Revelation, the idea of discipleship, encapsulated within the story of the seed, saturates the Scriptures.

God's first command to His original creation (Adam and Eve) and Christ's last command to His new creation (the church) are very similar (Gen. 1:28; Matt. 28:19-20). Both present an exhortation to spread godly seed throughout the earth. One may be tempted to gloss over that last sentence, but its significance is earth shattering. The God of the universe has charged His own to reproduce and cover the entire earth with His seed.

In Genesis 1:28 God commands Adam and Eve to "be fruitful and multiply and fill the earth." In Matthew 28:19-20, God commands His church to "make disciples of all nations." Those commands are similar in both form and function.

Adam and Eve were in the Garden of Eden, created perfect by God in His image to be the children of God. It is in this existence that God commissions them to reproduce and fill the earth. Likewise, the disciples were on the mountain, regenerated with a new nature by God to be the people of God. It is in this existence that Jesus commissions them to reproduce and fill the earth. "The risen Jesus has been given all authority in heaven and on earth, and so his followers are now to go and make disciples of all nations."[5]

Robert B. Chisholm Jr. offers the following paraphrase for Genesis 1:28: "Have a lot of children and populate the earth! Harness its potential and use its resources for your benefit."[6] Yet, this text is about more than merely having children. Genesis states that Adam and Eve were created in God's image. Claus Westermann expounds upon this profound reality:

> God intends to create human beings "according to our image, like ourselves." The question of what that means has been asked again and again. It does not mean a particular human quality; it is not an isolated assertion about human beings, but rather concerns the purpose of their creation. The Creator wants to create a being analogous to himself, to whom he can speak, who will listen and speak to him.[7]

One cannot minimize the state in which Adam and Eve received the command of God to "be fruitful and multiply and fill the earth, and subdue it" (Gen. 1:28). They were sinless. They had a perfect relationship with God. In that state God commanded them to reproduce. Just five chapters later, however, God felt very differently about the human race and the reproduction that followed.

> *Then the LORD saw that the wickedness of man was great on the earth, and that every intent of the thoughts of his heart was only evil continually. The LORD was sorry that He had made man on the earth, and He was grieved in His heart. The LORD said, "I will blot out man whom I have created from the face of the land, from man to animals to creeping things and to birds of the sky; for I am sorry that I have made them."*
>
> Genesis 6:5-7

These verses inform us that God did not want people simply to reproduce. God destroyed humanity through the global flood when it reproduced wickedness. God is grieved when people reproduce wickedness. When that happens, people cannot properly fulfill the latter part of Genesis 1:28 to "fill the earth, and subdue it; and rule over the fish of the sea and over the birds of the sky and over every living thing that moves on the earth." Rather, humanity will abuse the earth and as Genesis 6 attests, "every intent of the thoughts of his heart" will be evil.

On the contrary, God's desire is that people reproduce those who fear and follow Him (2 Peter 3:9). God's command for people to reproduce in Genesis 1:28 is much different from God's command for animals to reproduce in Genesis 1:22. "Whereas v. 22 simply gives a command, this verse (v. 28) adds 'and God said to them,' thus drawing attention to the personal relationship between God and man. [Humanity] is here commissioned to rule nature as a benevolent king, acting as God's representative over them and therefore treating them in the same way as God who created them."[8] The Great Commission in Matthew is a restatement of God's original desire and command to Adam and Eve in Genesis.

God is passionate about the spread of His seed throughout the earth. He desires that the whole earth be filled with His knowledge and glory (Habakkuk 2:14). Because humans are created as image bearers, they have the potential to participate in filling the earth with God's glory. Isaiah explained that those called of God are created for the purpose of glorifying Him. "Everyone who is called by My name, And whom I have created for My glory/ Whom I have formed, even whom I have made" (Isaiah 43:7).

What is so special about a seed? Why would I suggest that spreading godly seed is *the* main thrust of the Scriptures? Am I simply trying to create a seed hermeneutic or is it already there? Has God wrapped something special within the story of the seed?

Seeds are curious things, to say the least. I suppose it is because they contain a certain type of magic. What other element has within it the potential to reproduce life? Every thing created by human hands, no matter how technical, falls far short of seeds because it lacks the ability to reproduce itself. Regardless of whether people create cars, sweaters, houses, or pairs of shoes, none of these items will ever be able to reproduce itself.

Seeds are much different. A seed represents endless potential. In a single seed millions of other seeds reside, represented in life cycle after life cycle. The capability to feed a victimized nation or the potential to fill a vast forest dwells within a single seed. All of humanity came from one seed, Adam's sperm fertilized within Eve's womb.

## Usage of "Seed"

Before we examine "seed" in relation to discipleship, let us first look at how the word is used in the Bible. In the Old Testament "seed" was used in a variety of ways: 1) in a literal sense as a seed planted; 2) as semen; 3) offspring; 4) persons of quality.[9, 10]

The New Testament also uses "seed" with different connotations: 1) the seed from which anything springs; 2) semen and its produce (e.g. child, offspring, race); 3) whatever possesses life-force.[11]

The Gospels record Christ's parable of the sower where the Word itself is likened to a seed. Upon "the basis of Jesus' identification of the *sperma* with the 'Word of God' it is symbolic of the proclamation of the arrival of the kingdom."[12]

## The Existence of Two Seeds

Throughout the Scriptures God says some profound things in reference to "seed." In Genesis 1:28, He indirectly commissions Adam and Eve to spread His godly seed throughout the entire earth. Just two chapters later, in Genesis 3:15, however, we see that really two different seeds exist. We begin to understand that these two seeds have been striving against each other throughout the ages.

Immediately following the fall of humankind, God makes some significant statements to the serpent and to Eve about their future seeds. "And I will put enmity between you and the woman, And between your seed and her seed; He shall bruise you on the head, And you shall bruise him on the heel" (Gen. 3:15). Looking back, we can see within this verse a foretelling of the Virgin Birth, Christ the Promised Seed, His sufferings on the cross, and the eventual downfall of Satan.

The Scriptures record a rivalry between the two seeds. "The 'seed' of the woman…carries an elegiac accent, for hostility to the serpent race implies an enduring threat."[13] This view does not see the universe as a cosmic dualism between good and evil. Rather, it believes humankind has the ability to choose whether to be part of the godly seed through the finished work of *the* seed on the cross.

"Now the promises were spoken to Abraham and to his seed. He does not say, 'And to seeds,' as referring to many, but rather to one, 'And to your seed,' that is, Christ" (Gal. 3:16). Christ knew this reality and predicted what would happen when He died. He used the analogy of the physical seed to illustrate the outcome of the spiritual seed. "Truly, truly, I say to you, unless a grain of wheat falls into the earth and dies, it remains by itself alone; but if it dies, it bears much fruit" (John 12:24). It is through saving faith in the finished work of Christ that we actually are regenerated with the seed of God.

It may be a perplexing thought that we are regenerated with the seed of God, but having divine seed is not a new concept. Humanity's ability to possess the godly seed is a biblical concept. "For you have been born again not of seed which is perishable but imperishable, that is, through the living and abiding word of God" (1 Peter 1:23). "No one who is born of God practices sin, because His seed abides in him; and he cannot sin, because he is born of God" (1 John 3:9).

"In 1 John 3:9 the *sperma* [seed] of God denotes God's power at work, the Holy Spirit working in the hearts of believers."[14] Yet it is much more than God at work in the hearts of His own. Going further, "*sperma* in the New Testament refers to the seed of God. It refers to the beginning or germ of a new life, planted in us by the Spirit of God."[15]

The seed hermeneutic goes much further than a few individuals who trust in Him. In addition, the entire kingdom is likened to a seed (Matt. 13:31-32; Mark 4:26-34; Luke 13:18-21). We, His seed, will one day serve our King within His kingdom. "This then is the culmination of the theme we have noted throughout the Gospel, the calling of a people of God far wider than that of the Old Testament, in which membership is based not on race but on a relationship with God through his Messiah."[16] Therefore, in summary, Christ *the* seed bought us with His own blood in order that we might become *His* seed, so that we will be part of His kingdom, which is likened to a seed. "Posterity (*zera*) will serve Him; it will be told of the Lord to the coming generation" (Psalm 22:30).

We are witnessing an evolving seed hermeneutic. "As the physical *sperma* was the generator of life in the physical order (Gen. 1:11), so the divine *sperma* becomes the fount and origin of life in the new order of recreated humanity."[17]

## The Godly Seed

Scripture makes it clear that being born of godly seed has nothing to do with nationality. The Jews were proud about their nationality, but wrongfully so. "Nor are they all children because they are Abraham's descendants, but: 'through Isaac your descendants will be named.' That is, it is not the children of the flesh who are children of God, but the children of the promise are regarded as descendants" (Romans 7-8).

Although being a Jew still qualifies an individual as part of God's chosen people, like anyone else, a Jew needs to be regenerated by faith in Jesus Christ. "For this reason it is by faith, that it might be in accordance with grace, so that the promise will be guaranteed to all the descendants, not only to those who are of the Law, but also to those who are of the faith of Abraham, who is the father of us all" (Rom. 4:16). Thus, "when Paul uses *sperma* in regard to the Abrahamic line he has several different concepts in mind."[18] At times Pauline literature refers to the seed of Abraham as a physical thing only, i.e. being a Jew. At other times Pauline literature reflects the seed of Abraham as the true seed, i.e. regeneration. "And if you belong to Christ, then you are Abraham's descendants, heirs according to promise" (Gal. 3:29).

## The Ungodly Seed

Just as real as the existence of a godly seed is the existence of an ungodly seed. God identifies this seed as the seed of Satan (Gen. 3:15). Although it appears first in Genesis, the Scriptures are rich with other examples of the ungodly seed, often contrasted with the godly seed. "For the LORD loves justice, And does not forsake His godly ones; They are preserved forever; But the descendants of the wicked will be cut off" (Psalm 37:28). "Descendants" is another word for the Hebrew "seed."

With utmost clarity, Jesus classifies the Pharisees as part of the ungodly seed. He names the father of that seed as the devil himself. "You are of your father the devil, and you want to do the desires of your father" (John 8:44).

In His parables, Jesus acknowledges the existence of the godly and ungodly seed. He identifies Himself as the one sowing the good seed and Satan as the one sowing the ungodly seed. "The parable of the wheat and tares (Matt. 13:24-30), in which the Son of Man sows the seed of wheat (*sitos*) and the devil the seed of darnel (*zizanion*), affirms the simultaneous growth of good and evil during the present age."[19]

## Application of a Seed Hermeneutic

We must not let our hermeneutic exist without application. If we fail to apply, then quite simply we have failed. Most of us do not think much about seeds. We hold them in our hands without much enthusiasm. The problem is not with the seed, but with us. We are not forward thinkers. We are impressed with a piece of fruit, a flower, or a tree. Perhaps, it is what these things do for us, for the beauty they bring, or the nourishment they offer, that causes us to stand up and take notice. But a seed? Come on. A seed is just a seed.

Think for a moment about a seed. If you look at a single sperm through a microscope you may not think much of it. But when you realize that all humanity, all the inventions ever made, all art ever produced, all music ever composed, all thoughts ever thought, all tears ever cried this side of heaven came from God via a single sperm—that is an amazing concept!

Similarly, think about the church. The church was birthed from a single seed, Christ. As that single seed died, from Him came the church. We, the godly seed, all came from one. "Truly, truly, I say to you, unless a grain of wheat falls into the earth and dies, it remains alone; but if it dies, it bears much fruit" (John 12:24).

Within every true disciple lies the potential to reproduce an amazing number of additional disciples. The miracle of spiritual life is just that, a miracle. We cannot take credit for this miracle. We can only thank God that He has allowed us to play a part. Similarly, a man and woman cannot take credit for creating life. It is a gift. Yet, they are allowed to play a part in the reproduction of physical life.

We need to recognize our role in God's grand plan. If we fail to see the main plot, then we will fail to understand our role. The Lord commanded us to "go…make disciples of all the nations, baptizing them in the name of the Father and the Son and the Holy Spirit, teaching them to observe all that I commanded you " (Matt. 28:19-20).

Spreading the godly seed is evangelism. God longs for all to be regenerated (1 Tim. 2:4; 2 Peter 3:9). We cannot stop at evangelism, however. Even when people are regenerated, we cannot stop there. God commissioned us to make disciples, not merely converts.

We have seen the tremendous potential for one small seed to impact the world. But for any seed to have impact, of course, it must grow, mature, and bear many more seeds that will also grow, mature, and bear seeds. That process is called discipleship.

Seeds are magic. I think God made seeds like this on purpose. Within a seed lies a great mystery. A seed is so simple and yet so profound. For a seed to multiply, it must die. Many times throughout history, the ungodly seed has attempted, but failed, to kill the godly seed. From these attempted murders, the godly seed has come back with more force.

In the end, each regenerated one should feel great humility. I am humbled to know I am part of a much larger story. I am humbled that God has chosen me to be part of His godly seed. I am humbled that *the* seed died for me. And I am humbled that God has commissioned me to reproduce His seed within the hearts of others.

> *What is the kingdom of God like, and to what shall I compare it? It is like a mustard seed, which a man took and threw into his own garden; and it grew and became a tree; and the birds of the air nested in its branches.*
>
> Luke 13:18-19

# Relevant Verses

**Knowing/Theology** – Leviticus 19:37; Deuteronomy 5:1,27; 6:1-2; 7:12; 8:1; 10:12-13; 12:28; 13:4; 15:5; 17:11,18-20; 30:8,16; 31:11-12; 32:2,44-46; Joshua 8:34; 22:5; 24:26-27; Judges 2:10; 1 Samuel 2:3; 1 Kings 8:26; 18:18; 2 Kings 3:12; 8:2; 10:30-31; 11:4,9; 17:13,15,34,37; 18:6,12; 21:8; 22:11,13; 23:2-3,25 1 Chronicles 10:13; 22:12,13,19; 28:6-10; 29:19; 2 Chronicles 1:10; Ezra 7:10; Nehemiah 8:9-12; Job 21:14; Proverbs 1:3, 22,29; Isaiah 29:13; Ezekiel 2:7; 3:10; 5:6; 11:12; 20:11,13,16,18,19,21,24; 28:23-24; 33:31; 34:27; 36:26-27; 37:24; Daniel 2:21; 9:3; Amos 2:4; Hosea 1:1; 2:20; 4:6,14; 5:4-5; 6:3, 6; 13:4; 14:9; Micah 2:7; 4:2,5; 6:8; Habakkuk 2:14; Malachi 2:6-8; 4:4; Luke 6:46-49; 8:21; 11:28; John 1:26; 4:8,20; 8:37,51,54-55; 10:14; 13:17; 15:14; 17:8,14; Acts 1:1; 13:15, 44, 49; 14:3,7,15; 15:21,35; 16:32; 17:2,11; 18:5,11,23-25,26,28; 19:8,9-10,20; Romans 1:32; 6:6,17; 10:2-3,17; 15:18; 1 Corinthians 4:17; 5:2; 8:1; 2 Corinthians 5:11; Galatians 4:9; Ephesians 4:1,21; Philippians 1:9; 4:9; Colossians 1:5,28; 2:2; 3:10; 1 Thessalonians 4:2,5; 2 Thessalonians 3:1; 1 Timothy 4:6,12,16; 6:2,17; 2 Timothy 4:15; Titus 1:3,9,16; 2:1,3,5,10,15; Philemon 1:6; Hebrews 5:12; 8:10; 10:26; James 1:18,23-24; 2:8,17; 4:17; 1 Peter 1:23,25; 2:8; 2 Peter 1:2,3,5,6,8 2:12,20; 1 John 1:1,6; 2:3,6,7,8,13,14,21,27 3:1,6; 4:7-8; 5:13,20; 2 John 2:1,9,10; Revelation 1:3; 2:24; 3:3

**Being/Spiritual Formation** – Deuteronomy 5:1,27; 6:6,17; 7:12; 8:6; 10:12-13; 11:1,8,13,22; 13:4; 17:19-20; 26:16-18; 30:1,8,14,16; 31:11-12; 32:44-46; Joshua 1:7-8; 22:5; 23:11; 1 Samuel 12:24; 1 Kings 2:4; 8:23,25,58,61; 9:4-6; 10:24; 11:33,38; 14:8; 15:3; 2 Kings 10:30-31; 20:3; 23:25; 1 Chronicles 28:6-10; 29:19; Ezra 7:10; Isaiah 29:13; Ezekiel 3:10; 11:12,19-20; 33:31; 36:26-27; 37:24; Daniel 4:9,18; 5:14; 6:3; 9:3; 11:12; Hosea 5:4-5; 7:2; Zechariah 1:6; 7:12; 12:1; Malachi 2:6-7; 3:3; Matthew 12:33; John 6:45; 17:23; Romans 2:20; 6:17; 10:10; Galatians 3:2; Philippians 2:13; Colossians 3:10; 1 Timothy 1:5; 4:11-13,16; 5:7; 6:3,11; Philemon 1:5; Hebrews 5:12; 6:1-3; 8:10; James 1:25; 1 Peter 1:4.15-16,22; 1 John 1:6; 2:3,6,7,8,13,14,24; 3:17,24; 4:13,15; 2 John 1:2,9; Revelation 1:3; 3:3;

**Doing/Ministry** – Leviticus 19:37; Deuteronomy 5:1; 6:1-3,17-18,25; 7:12; 8:1; 10:12-13; 11:22,32; 12:14,28,31-32; 13:4; 15:5; 17:10,18-20; 26:16-18; 27:10,26; 28:1,9,13,15, 45; 29:9,29; 30:16; 31:11-12; 32:44-46; Joshua 1:8; 22:5; 23:6; Judges 2:17; 13:14; Ruth 2:11; 1 Samuel 8:3,5; 12:25; 13:13; 2 Samuel 2:6; 7:3,25; 1 Kings 2:3,4; 3:14; 6:12-13; 7:14; 9:4-6; 15:11,26,34; 16:19,25,30; 21:20,25-26; 22:43,52; 2 Kings 3:2; 8:18; 10:30-31; 13:2,11; 14:3,24; 15:3,9,18,21, 24,28,31,34,36; 16:2-3,16,19; 17:2,9,13,17,34,40; 18:3,6; 20:3,20; 21:2,8-9,19-21; 22:2,7,13; 23:25,32,37; 24:9,19; 1 Chronicles 10:13; 21:17; 22:13,19; 28:6-10; 29:19; Ezra 7:10; Isaiah 1:13-17; 29:13; Ezekiel 5:6; 11:12; 18:9,14,17,24; 20:11,13,16,18,19,21,24; 22:9; 23:37; 33:31; 36:26-27; 37:24; Daniel 4:27; 7:27; 9:5,10; Hosea 5:4-5; 7:2; 12:2; 14:9 Amos 2:4; 5:21-24; Jonah 1:10; 3:10; Micah 2:7; 3:4; 4:2,5; 6:8; Zechariah 1:4; 3:7; 7:9; 10:12; Malachi 2:6-7,17; Matthew 11:19; Luke 6:46-49; 8:21; 11:28; John 3:19-21; 7:7; 8:39; 13:15,17; 14:15,21,23; 15:14; 1 John 2:6; 3:17; 4:20; 5:2-3; Acts 1:1; 10:35; Romans 1:32; 2:1-3,13; 13:3,12; 15:18; 1 Corinthians 7:17; 11:24; 15:58; 16:10; 2 Corinthians 5:18; 11:12; 13:7-8; Galatians 6:9,16; Ephesians 5:2,8,11; 6:9; Philippians 1:27; 2:13; 4:9; Colossians 1:10; 3:7,23; 4:5; 1

Timothy 3:15; 1 Timothy 4:12,16; 5:10,25; Titus 1:16; 3:14; Philemon 1:14,21; Hebrews 6:10; 10:7,24,36; 11:33; James 1:22,23,25,27; 2:8,17,26; 3:13; 4:17; 1 Peter 1:15,17,22; 2:12; 3:2,6,11,17; 4:10,17,18; 2 Peter 2:8; 3:11,17; 1 John 1:6; 2:9,11,29; 3:7,8,9,10,12,14,18,22; 2 John. 1:4,6,11; 2:6,11; 3 John 1:3,4,10,11,12; Revelation 1:3; 2:5,8,23; 3:2-3,8,15-16; 7:15; 12:17; 14:13,17; 15:4; 17:2; 20:12-13; 22:3,7,11;

**Reproducing/Coaching** – Deuteronomy 6:1-2,7,20; 7:12-13a; 8:1; 11:18-19; 12:28; 17:10,18-20; 29:29; 30:16; 31:11-12; 32:44-46; 1 Samuel 8:3,5; 1 Kings 2:4; 3:14; 6:13; 9:6; 11:6,33,38; 14:9,22,24; 15:26,34; 16:19,25,30; 2 Kings 3:2; 8:18; 10:30-31; 13:2,11; 14:3,24; 15:3,9,18,24,28,31,34; 16:2; 17:2,13,17,40; 18:6; 21:8,20-21; 22:2,13; 23:32,37; 24:9,19; 1 Chronicles 28:6-10; 29:19; Ezra 7:10; Ezekiel 11:12; Hosea 5:4-5; Joel 1:3; Amos 2:4; Zechariah 7:9; Malachi 2:6-8; Matthew 10:14,24-25; 28:19-20; John 13:15; 17:20; Acts 1:1; 5:21,25,28,42; 10:38; 26:28; Romans 1:32; 1 Corinthians 4:17; 16:10; 2 Corinthians 5:11; Galatians 6:6; Philippians 1:14; 3:17; Colossians 1:7,28; 1 Timothy 4:6,12,16; 6:2,17; 2 Timothy 2:2; Titus 1:9; 2:15; Hebrews 5:12; 6:12; James 3:1; 1 John 1:1-3; Revelation 1:3

# Endnotes

## Introduction

1. <http://explorersfoundation.org/glyphery/122.html> accessed October 26, 2006.

## Chapter 1

1. Matthew 28:19-20
2. Matthew 22:37
3. Galatians 4:19
4. Romans 12:2
5. John 17:18
6. 1 Corinthians 12:27
7. John 10:10
8. Matthew 10:37-39; Luke 14:25-35; John 12:24-25; Romans 8:13; 1 Corinthians 15:31
9. Luke 14:25-35
10. 1 Corinthians 9:24-27; Galatians 2:20
11. Matthew 22:14

## Chapter 2

1. <www.reformed.org/documents/larger1.html> accessed October 15, 2005.
2. John 15:8

3. C. S. Lewis, *Mere Christianity* (New York: Macmillan Publishing, Co., 1978) pp .169, 171.
4. Habakkuk 2:14

## Chapter 3

1. Matthew 4:19; Matthew 9:9
2. Matthew 8:19
3. Matthew 8:20
4. Matthew 8:21
5. Matthew 8:22
6. Luke 9:23
7. Matthew 8:23
8. Luke 9:49, 54; John 18:10
9. There were several important centers of fishing and fish industry along the shore of Lake Tiberias, as attested by the names Bethsaida ("house of fishing"), Magdala ("bulwark of the fishes"), and Tarichaea ("salting installation for fish"). Bromiley.
10. Matthew 4:19
11. Matthew 4:19. Luke adds more detail in Luke 5:1-11 where Jesus performs a miracle with fish that authenticates the authority of His call in the preceding verses. It is the result of this miracle catch that Peter, James, and John (Andrew not mentioned) leave all they know to follow the one that knows them. Douglass R. Hare, *Matthew (Interpretation, a Bible Commentary for Teaching and Preaching)* (Louisville: John Knox Press, 1993) pp. 29-30.
12. Matthew 19:27
13. John 1:43
14. Matthew 9:9-17
15. Philippians 3:8 (KJV)
16. John 21:3

## Chapter 4

1. 2 Corinthians 13:5

2. Reading for Philosophical Inquiry, *Main Divisions of Philosophy*, <http://philosophy.lander.edu/intro/introbook2.1/x924.html> accessed January 22, 2006.
3. Acts 15:18; Psalm 147:4
4. Psalm 139:7-12
5. Genesis 17:1; Exodus 6:3; 2 Corinthians 6:18; Revelation 1:8; 19:6
6. Matthew 10:1, 4
7. John 6:70-71; John 17:12
8. Mathew 26:21-23
9. John 13:27-29
10. James 2:19
11. 2 Corinthians 13:5
12. 1 John 5:13-14

## Chapter 5

1. 1 Corinthians 8:1
2. 2 Timothy 3:7
3. 1 Timothy 1:4; 4:7; 2 Timothy 4:4; Titus 1:14; 2 Peter 1:16
4. Matthew 18:3
5. Hebrews 5:11-6:2
6. Hebrews 5:12
7. Acts 16:16-18; James 2:19
8. John 5:39; 1 Corinthians 13:2; 2 Timothy 3:7

## Chapter 6

1. Tim Vivian, *Journeying into God: Seven Early Monastic Lives.* (Minneapolis: Fortress Press, 1996) p. 1.
2. Basil M. Pennington and Nicolas Sapieha, *Monastery: Prayer, Work, Community* (San Francisco: Harper & Row Publishers,) p. 105.
3. Ibid. p. 18.
4. John Binns, *Ascetics and Ambassadors of Christ: The Monasteries of Palestine, 314-631* (New York: Oxford University Press, 1994) p. 79.

5. Simon Peter Iredale, *The Interior Mountain: Encountering God with the Desert Saints*. (Nashville: Abingdon Press, 2000) p. 9.
6. Doug Pagitt, *Reimagining Spiritual Formation: A Week in the Life of an Experimental Church* (Grand Rapids: Zondervan Publishing House, 2003) p. 119.
7. Philippians 1:6

## Chapter 7

1. Luke 8:21
2. John 15:14
3. John 13:17; Luke 11:28
4. Marvin R Wilson, *Our Father Abraham: Jewish Roots of the Christian Faith* (Grand Rapids: Wm. B. Eerdmans Publishing Co, 1989) p. 279.
5. Ibid., p. 287.
6. 1 Corinthians 11:24
7. Luke 6:46
8. Revelation 3:15-16
9. John 13:35
10. 1 John 4:8
11. Romans 10:17
12. 2 Peter 1:4
13. Galatians 5:16
14. Philippians 4:13
15. Galatians 2:20
16. Romans 6:6
17. 1 Corinthians 9:27
18. James 2:17
19. Bill Thrall, Bruce McNicol, and Ken McElrath, *The Ascent of a Leader: How Ordinary Relationships Develop Extraordinary Character and Influence* (San Francisco: Jossey-Bass, 1999) pp. 101-102.
20. Wilson, p. 287.
21. "Sacred vs. Secular," Rocky Mountain Family Council, <http://www.rmfc.org/fs/fs0023.html> accessed October 21, 2005.
22. <www.redeemer.on.ca/academics/polisci/kuyper.html> accessed October 24, 2005.

## Chapter 8

1. Genesis 1:11-12
2. Romans 8:1; Ephesians 1:6; 1 John 4:18

## Chapter 9

1. Matthew 10:1-5; Luke 6:16; John 17:12
2. 1 Timothy 1:20; 2 Timothy 4:14
3. Luke 18:17-24
4. Matthew 22:35-41
5. 2 Corinthians 13:5
6. 1 Corinthians 1:12; 3:4-6, 22; 4:6; 16:12; Titus 3:13
7. Philippians 3:5-6
8. Acts 9
9. Bill Hull, *The Disciple-Making Church* (Old Tappan, N.J.: Fleming H. Revell Company, 1990).
10. C. Christopher Smith, *Water, Faith & Wood: Stories of the Early Church's Witness for Today* (Indianapolis: Doulos Christou Press, 2003).
11. Darrell L. Guder, *The Continuing Conversion of the Church* (Grand Rapids: Wm. B. Eerdmans Publishing Co., 2000).
12. Matthew 7:21
13. 1 Corinthians 13:3
14. Matthew 7:15
15. Matthew 7:21-23
16. Marvin R. Wilson, *Our Father Abraham: Jewish Roots of the Christian Faith* (Grand Rapids: Wm. B. Eerdmans Publishing Co, 1989) p. 287.
17. Hosea 5:4
18. James 1:23-24
19. William L. Banks, *In Search of the Great Commission: What did Jesus Really Say?* (Chicago: Moody Press, 1991).

## Chapter 10

1. Alice Fryling, *Disciplemakers' Handbook* (Downers Grove, Ill.: InterVarsity Press, 1989) p. 19.

## Chapter 11

1. Os Guinness, *Fit Bodies Fat Minds: Why Evangelicals Don't Think and What to do About it* (Grand Rapids: Baker Books, 1994) pp. 18-19.
2. C. Christopher Smith, *Water, Faith & Wood: Stories of the Early Church's Witness for Today* (Indianapolis: Doulos Christou Press, 2003), p. 39.
3. "An Introduction to the School of Alexandria," Coptic Orthodox Church Network, <www.copticchurch.net/topics/patrology/schoolsofalex/1-Intro/chapter1.html> accessed March 18, 2005.
4. Joseph C. Hough, Jr., *The Marginalization of Theology in the University: Religious Studies, Theological Studies and the University-Divinity School.* ed. Joseph Mitsuo Kitagawa (Atlanta: Scholars Press, 1992) p. 48.
5. Edward Farley, *Theologia: The Fragmentation and Unity of Theological Education* (Eugene, Ore.: Wipf and Stock Publishers, 1994) p. 197.
6. Terence J. Martin, Jr., *Theology as University: Erasmus' Conversational Imperative*, The Annual Publication of the College Theology Society, ed. John Apczynski, vol. 33 (Lanham, Md.: University Press of America, Inc., 1990) p. 50.
7. Ibid. p. 49
8. Hough, p. 47
9. Martin, p. 51
10. George Bernard Shaw <www.writersalmanac.publicradio.org/programs/2003/07/21/index. html>, accessed September 24, 2006.
11. 2 Corinthians 10:5
12. <www.answers.google.com/answers/threadview?id=56750>, accessed November 7, 2005.
13. Quoted by John C. Maxwell, "Avoiding Mental Flabbiness," <http://inspiredgrowth.org/maxwell_mentalflab.htm>, accessed September 24, 2006.
14. Craig R Thompson, ed, trans. *The Colloquies of Erasmus* (Chicago: University of Chicago, 1965), p. 630.
15. Farley, p. 197

16. Robert Banks, *Reenvisioning Theological Education: Exploring a Missional Alternative to Current Models* (Grand Rapids: Wm. B. Eerdmans Publishing Co., 1999) pp. 58-59.
17. Wilson Yates, *The Arts in Theological Education: New Possibilities for Integration* (Atlanta: Scholars Press, 1987) p. 6.
18. 1 Kings 7:4, 5; 2 Chronicles 3:10
19. Exodus 31:1-11; 35:31-35
20. Yates, p. 1
21. Ibid., p. 10
22. Edgar J. Elliston and J. Timothy Kauffman, *Developing Leaders for Urban Ministries* (New York: Peter Lang, 1993) pp. 116-117.
23. Banks, p. 157
24. Oswald Chambers, *My Utmost for His Highest*. (New York: Dodd, Mead, and Company, 1935), p. 166.
25. Guinness, p. 140
26. Robert E. Webber, *Ancient-Future Faith: Rethinking Evangelicalism for a Postmodern World* (Grand Rapids: Baker Books, 1999) p 163.
27. Doug Pagitt, *Reimagining Spiritual Formation: A Week in the Life of an Experimental Church* (Grand Rapids: Zondervan Publishing House, 2003) p. 23.
28. Webber, p. 156
29. Loc. cit.
30. Wilson, p. 301
31. Quoted in Russell W. West, "When Seminary Goes to Church: Church-Based Theological Education as Leadership Formation Partner" (Academy of Religious Leadership: Annual Papers: 2004) p. 20.
32. Wilson, p. 156
33. Banks, p. 19
34. quoted by Ronald W. Richardson, *Creating a Healthier Church: Family Systems Theory, Leadership, and Congregational Life* (Knoxville: Fortress Press, 1996) p. 105.
35. Parker J. Palmer, *To Know as We Are Known: A Spirituality of Education* (San Francisco: Harper & Row, 1982) p. 42.
36. Webber, p. 156

37. Larry Crabb, *The Safest Place on Earth: Where People Connect and Are Forever Changed* (Nashville: W Publishing Group, 1999) p. 4.
38. John 17:17
39. <http://www.gbcpowell.org/youthministry.html>, accessed November 11, 2005
40. Farley
41. Banks, pp. 58-59

## Chapter 12

1. Ken Hutcherson, *Here Comes the Bride: The Church: What We are Meant to Be* (Sisters, Ore.: Multnomah Books, 1998) p. 47.
2. Darrell L. Guder, *The Continuing Conversion of the Church* (Grand Rapids: Wm. B. Eerdmans Publishing Co., 2000) p. 26.
3. Robert E. Quinn, *Deep Change: Discovering the Leader Within* (San Francisco: Jossey-Bass, 1996) p. 25.
4. Luke 9:23
5. John Driver, *Images of the Church in Mission* (Scottsdale, Pa.: Herald Press, 1997) p. 21.
6. Jim Herrington, Mike Bonem, and James H. Furr, *Leading Congregational Change: A Practical Guide for the Transforming Journey* (San Francisco: Jossey-Bass, 2000), p. xiii.
7. James M. Kouzes and Barry Z. Posner, *Credibility: How Leaders Gain and Lose It, Why People Demand it* (San Francisco: Jossey-Bass, 1993) p. 249.
8. Matthew 11:12, NIV
9. Douglas J. Rumford, *Soul Shaping: Taking Care of your Spiritual Life* (Wheaton: Tyndale House), p. 65.
10. Charles R. Swindoll, *Active Spirituality: A Non-Devotional Guide* (Dallas: Word Publishing, 1994) p. xi.
11. Thomas W. Ogletree, "Dimensions of Practical Theology: Some Reflections on the Relation of Theory and Practice" in *Integration: Objective Studies and Practical Theology*, Report of the sixteenth biennial meeting of the association for professional education for ministry held in Colorado 14-16 June 1980, edited by Robert L. Browning. (Denver: University of Denver, 1980) p. 9.

12. Robert E. Webber, *Ancient-Future Faith: Rethinking Evangelicalism for a Postmodern World* (Grand Rapids: Baker Books, 1999) p. 156.
13. Quinn, pp. 3-4.
14. Susan Annette Muto, *A Practical Guide to Spiritual Reading* (Petersham, Mass.: St. Bede's Publications, 1994) p. 57.
15. Herrington et. al., p. 18
16. Ron DelBene and Herb Montgomery, *The Breath of Life: A Simple Way to Pray* (Minneapolis: Winston Press, 1981) p. 27.
17. John Bunyan, *Prayer* (Aylesbury, England: Hazell Watson & Viney Ltd., 1965) p. 13.
18. Ivan H. French, *The Principles and Practice of Prayer*, Reprint (Winona Lake, Ind.: BMH Books, 1997) pp. 15-18.
19. John 5:19
20. Matthew 5:3
21. Robert C. Bondi, *In Ordinary Time: Healing the Wounds of the Heart* (Nashville: Abingdon Press, 1996) p. 45.
22. <www.webster.com/dictionary/importunate>, accessed October 19, 2006.
23. Edgar J. Elliston and J. Timothy Kauffman, *Developing Leaders for Urban Ministries* (New York: Peter Lang, 1993).

## Chapter 13

1. C. Christopher Smith, *Water, Faith & Wood: Stories of the Early Church's Witness for Today* (Indianapolis: Doulos Christou Press, 2003) p. 30.
2. Ray S. Anderson, "Theologians in Thought and Life" in *Education for Ministry: Theology, Preparedness, Praxis.* Report of the Fifteenth Biennial Meeting of the Association for Professional Education for Ministry Held in Canada 17-19 June 1978, edited by Gaylord B. Noyce (Toronto, Ontario: Trinity College, 1978) p. 26.
3. Ibid. p. 26.
4. Luke 4:43-44
5. Luke 5:16; 6:12, 28; 9:28
6. Edgar J. Elliston and J. Timothy Kauffman, *Developing Leaders for Urban Ministries* (New York: Peter Lang, 1993) p. 201.

7. Anderson, p. 26
8. John Driver, *Images of the Church in Mission* (Scottsdale, Pa.: Herald Press, 1997) p. 94.
9. Barbara Wheeler and Edward Farley, eds. *Shifting Boundaries: Contextual Approaches to the Structure of Theological Education* (Louisville: Westminster/John Knox, 1991) p. 9.
10. John Binns, *Ascetics and Ambassadors of Christ: The Monasteries of Palestine, 314-631* (New York: Oxford University Press, 1994) p. 96-97.
11. Doug Pagitt, *Reimagining Spiritual Formation: A Week in the Life of an Experimental Church* (Grand Rapids: Zondervan Publishing House, 2003) p. 31.
12. Robert Banks, *Reenvisioning Theological Education: Exploring a Missional Alternative to Current Models* (Grand Rapids: Wm. B. Eerdmans Publishing Co., 1999) p. 29.
13. James 1:27


## Chapter 14


1. Robert Banks, *Reenvisioning Theological Education: Exploring a Missional Alternative to Current Models* (Grand Rapids: Wm. B. Eerdmans Publishing Co., 1999) p. 113.
2. Marvin R. Wilson, *Our Father Abraham: Jewish Roots of the Christian Faith* (Grand Rapids: Wm. B. Eerdmans Publishing Co., 1989) p. 301.
3. Proverbs 15:22
4. "Pontifications," <*http://catholica.pontifications.net/?p=274*>, accessed January 22, 2006.
5. C. Christopher Smith, *Water, Faith & Wood: Stories of the Early Church's Witness for Today* (Indianapolis: Doulos Christou Press, 2003) p. 30
6. Banks, p. 172
7. Larry Crabb, *The Safest Place on Earth: Where People Connect and are Forever Changed* (Nashville: W Publishing Group, 1999) p. 81.
8. Ronald W. Richardson, *Creating a Healthier Church: Family Systems Theory, Leadership, and Congregational Life.* (Minneapolis: Fortress Press, 1996) p. 25.
9. Proverbs 27:17

10. Banks, pp. 85-86
11. Gunter Krallman, *Mentoring for Missions: Leadership Principles Exemplified by Jesus Christ.* (Hong Kong: Jensco Limited, 1992) p. 32.
12. Russell W. West, *When Seminary Goes to Church: Church-Based Theological Education as Leadership Formation Partner* (Academy of Religious Leadership Annual Papers, 2004) p. 5.
13. Ibid. p. 7.
14. A. B. Bruce, *The Training of the Twelve* (Grand Rapids: Kregel, 1988) p. 6.
15. Mark 6:41-43
16. Luke 10:9
17. Banks, pp. 87-88
18. Jean Leclercq, *The Love of Learning and the Desire for God* (New York: Fordham University Press, 1961) p. 3.
19. Stanley Soltau, *Missions at the Crossroads* (Grand Rapids: Baker Books, 1955) p. 16.
20. Banks, pp. 90-91.
21. J. Hebert Kane, *Understanding Christian Missions* (Grand Rapids: Baker Books, 1974), p. 122.
22. Crabb, p. 30
23. Doug Pagitt, *Reimagining Spiritual Formation: A Week in the Life of an Experimental Church* (Grand Rapids: Zondervan, 2003), p. 26.
24. Jean Vanier, *Brokenness to Community* (Mahwah, NJ.: Paulist Press 1992) p. 40.
25. Crabb, p. 45

## Chapter 15

1. 1 Corinthians 13:2
2. John Driver, *Images of the Church in Mission* (Scottsdale, Pa.: Herald Press), p. 37.
3. Os Guinness, *Fit Bodies Fat Minds: Why Evangelicals Don't Think and What to do About it* (Grand Rapids: Baker Books, 1994) p. 28.
4. Marvin R Wilson, *Our Father Abraham: Jewish Roots of the Christian Faith* (Grand Rapids: Wm. B. Eerdmans Publishing Co., 1989) pp. 289-290.

5. Ronald H. and Stanley P. Saunders, "Feet Partly of Iron and Partly of Clay: Pedagogy and the Curriculum of Theological Education," *Theological Education* 28, no.2 (Spring 1992), pp 44-45.
6. Andrew Kirk, *Theology and the Third World Church Outreach and Identity: Evangelical Theological Monographs*, ed. Bruce J. Nicholls, No. 6. (Downers Grove, Ill.: InterVarsity Press, 1983), p. 51.
7. Edward Farley, *Theologia: The Fragmentation and Unity of Theological Education* (Eugene Ore.: Wipf and Stock Publishers, 1994), p. 134.
8. Robert Banks, *Reenvisioning Theological Education: Exploring a Missional Alternative to Current Models* (Grand Rapids: Wm. B. Eerdmans Publishing Co., 1999), pp. 73-74.
9. James Orr, gen. ed. *The International Standard Bible Encyclopedia* (Grand Rapids: Wm. B. Eerdmans Publishing Co., 1939).
10. Farley, p. 52
11. William J. Webb, *Slaves, Women & Homosexuals: Exploring the Hermeneutics of Cultural Analysis* (Downers Grove, Ill.: InterVarsity Press, 2001), p. 22.
12. Edgar J. Elliston and J. Timothy Kauffman, *Developing Leaders for Urban Ministries* (New York: Peter Lang, 1993), p. 164.
13. Dieumeme Noelliste, *Toward a Theology of Theological Education Outreach and Identity: Evangelical Theological Monographs*, ed. Bong Rin Ro, No. 10. (Seoul, South Korea: World Evangelical Fellowship Theological Commission, 1993), p. 15.
14. Robert E. Webber, *Ancient-Future Faith: Rethinking Evangelicalism for a Postmodern World* (Grand Rapids: Baker Books, 1999) p. 156.

## Chapter 16

1. Alice Fryling, *Disciplemakers' Handbook* (Downers Grove, Ill.: InterVarsity Press, 1989), p. 8.
2. C. S. Lewis, *Mere Christianity* (New York: Macmillan Publishing, 1978) pp .169, 171.
3. <www.breitbart.com/news/2005/10/30/D8DIM630N.html>, accessed November 23, 2005.

4. *Relevant Magazine*, January/February 2006 Issue 18.

## Appendix

1. Donald McKim, *The Bible in Theology & Preaching* (Eugene, Ore.: Wipf and Stock, 1999) p. 72.
2. Sarah Heaner Lancaster, *Women and the Authority of Scripture: A Narrative Approach* (Harrisburg, Pa.: Trinity Press Int'l. 2002) p. 32.
3. Malcolm Goldsmith, *Knowing Me Knowing God: Exploring Your Spirituality with Myers-Briggs* (Nashville: Abingdon Press, 1997) p. 37.
4. Robert M. Mulholland, *Shaped by the Word: the Power of Scripture in Spiritual Formation* (Nashville: Upper Room Books, 2000) p. 52.
5. R. T. France, *Matthew: Evangelist and Preacher* (Grand Rapids: Zondervan Publishing House, 1989) p. 235.
6. Robert B. Chisholm, Jr., *From Exegesis to Exposition: A Practical Guide to Using Biblical Hebrew* (Grand Rapids: Baker Books, 1998) p. 46.
7. Claus Westermann, *Genesis: A Practical Commentary* (Grand Rapids: Wm. B. Eerdmans Publishing Co., 1987) p. 10.
8. Gordon J. Wenham, *Word Biblical Commentary*, Vol. 1, Genesis 1-15 (Waco: Word Books, 1987) p. 33.
9. Francis Brown, S. R. Driver, and Charles A. Briggs, *A Hebrew and English Lexicon of the Old Testament*, Reprint (Peabody, Mass.: Hendrickson Publishers) p. 282.
10. R. Laird Harris, Gleason L. Archer, and Bruce K. Waltke, eds. *Theological Wordbook of the Old Testament*, Vol. 1, Aleph-Mem (Chicago: Moody Press, 1980) p. 252.
11. Joseph H. Thayer, *Thayer's Greek-English Lexicon of the New Testament*, Reprint (Peabody, Mass.: Hendrickson Publishers), p. 584.
12. Brown et. al., p. 522.
13. Gerhard Friedrich and Gerhard Kittel, eds. *Theological Dictionary of the New Testament*, Vol. 8, S. Trans. & ed. Geoffrey W. Bromiley (Grand Rapids: Wm. B. Eerdmans Publishing Co., 1971) p. 538.

14. Spiros Zodhiates, *The Complete Word Study of the New Testament* (Iowa Falls, Iowa: World Bible Publishers) p. 956.
15. Walter Bauer, *A Greek-English Lexicon of the New Testament and Other Early Christian Literature*, 4th rev. ed. Translated and edited by William F. Arndt and F. Wilbur Gingrich (Chicago and London: University of Chicago Press) p. 762.
16. France, p. 414.
17. Brown et. al., p. 524.
18. Zodhiates, p. 956.
19. Brown et. al., p. 523.

# CALLED Workbook

This 60-page booklet contains more than 150 carefully crafted questions that will help you get at what it means to live as an authentic follower of Jesus. As a complement to *CALLED*, the workbook will stimulate your spiritual life by enabling you to dig deeper. It also contains a generous amount of space for journaling and reflecting, which makes incarnation into everyday life easier. The workbook is an excellent aid to personal growth and can be used also in small groups along with *CALLED* as the study text. You can order the workbook at www.karyoberbrunner.com.

# Kary Oberbrunner

## Recovering Pharisee

### Why Recovering Pharisee?

**Recovering**—I believe every true follower of Jesus is in process. I use the word "recovering" to communicate the fact that I haven't arrived yet. I grew up in a strong Christian home, but slowly over time I exchanged a vibrant relationship with God for religious performance. Although I trusted Jesus Christ as my Lord and Savior, I strived to repay God's grace through duty and rules.

I felt as though my salvation and the weight of the world rested on my shoulders. These were dark times. I sank into years of depression.

**Pharisee**—Ironically during my time in seminary, I felt the farthest from God. It seemed as though I couldn't break through to Him. In reality, He was breaking through to me. God transcended my religion and the boxes I tried to keep Him in. His grace crushed me, literally. I came to the end of myself and in the process I finally began to find God.

I felt like a little kid, alive for the first time, in a world of mystery and wonder. I believe much of this life is God wooing us to Him, offering us abundant life *now*, through His Son Jesus Christ.

## Recovering Pharisee E-Newsletter

**WHAT IS IT?**

It's a tool.
It's a way to stay up-to-date.
It's a conversation.
It's a community.
It's biblically trustworthy.
It's culturally relevant.
It's what's touching the Church.
It's what's affecting the world.
It's late breaking.
It's emerging.

Sign-up today at KaryOberbrunner.com

# KaryOberbrunner

Below are some of the services that Kary Oberbrunner and Redeem the Day Ministries offer. Find out more information by visiting KaryOberbrunner.com

**Speaking**

Kary has spoken across the country in many settings including colleges, camps, and conferences. He has a heart for the local church and understands, from personal experience, the daily joys and struggles of vocational ministry. Kary is a published author and writes regularly for several magazines on such subjects as holiness, Christian living, and cultural phenomena.

Kary strives to use verbal and visual illustrations that drive home advanced spiritual principles. In church settings, he has frequently been told that his talks "connect" with eight-year-olds and eighty-year-olds. He "borrows" this style from Jesus' example in the Gospels.

**Workshops**

Kary works with churches, staffs, non-profits, and businesses to provide transformational workshops. Some of the most popular workshops include:

- Called: Authentically Following Jesus
- Journey Towards Relevance
- Who Am I?
- How to Bring Change in Your Church
- Visionary Leadership
- Unpacking Postmodernism
- Redeem the Day

### Coaching and Consulting

Every living thing encounters conflict. Individuals, ministries, and churches are not exceptions. Often our first reaction regarding conflict is to see it negatively. Yet, it's through conflict that growth occurs. The potential for reformation and revival is on the other side of every conflict. Although our natural tendency is to reject change, when just one person changes, an entire organization can be affected.

Kary received his Doctor of Ministry degree in Transformational Leadership. He balances his consulting and coaching approach by combining the academic with experience. He brings people and churches to a place to see God's agenda. With ultimate reliance on the Holy Spirit, Kary offers a path of spiritual formation that leads to transformation and practical incarnation.

# Biography

Dr. Kary Oberbrunner, self-proclaimed "Recovering Pharisee," is founder of Redeem the Day Ministries and serves as Director of Grace Institute and Pastor of Discipleship and Leadership Development at the Grace Brethren Church of Powell, Ohio. Through his speaking, writing, coaching, and consultation, he invites others into a holistic relationship with Jesus Christ.

Kary believes that we can grow in our faith only when we're real with where we are. He thinks God can handle our anger, frustration, and confusion, but that He won't tolerate our hypocrisy. Kary is a fresh voice of authenticity for this generation, calling others to live lives larger than themselves.

Kary has spoken across the country in many settings including colleges, camps, and conferences. He has a heart for the local church and understands, from personal experience, the daily joys and struggles of vocational ministry. Kary is a published author and writes regularly for several magazines on such subjects as holiness, Christian living, and cultural phenomena.

Kary is married to his soul mate Kelly. They are the proud parents of Keegan. In his free time Kary enjoys reading, the outdoors, discerning culture, and playing disc golf. Contact him at: KaryOberbrunner.com

# Grace Institute

Grace Institute is a model for leadership development that produces a community of life-long learners and laborers. It is a holistic way of learning derived from a Hebrew mindset of education. Our students are not measured exclusively upon their knowledge or grades. Rather, they are measured on their knowing, being, doing, and reproducing. We intentionally incarnate our theology. All of learning takes place within the context of experience and relationships. We do not "dumb down" theology. Rather, we strive to reproduce theologians in thought and life.

There is no dualism between the sacred and the secular. Thus, we view all of life as a continuum of potential worship of God. We worship Him in our mundane service just as much as in our biblical exegesis. We are evangelical. We are missional. We believe every vocation needs leaders who are holistically developed and who minister out of a deep reservoir of theology.

**Our Vision:** To equip and empower current and emerging leaders to grow as authentic followers of Jesus Christ.

**Our Mission:** To partner with individuals and ministries to provide teaching, training, coaching, and consultation.

**Our Paradigm:** The Grace Institute centers around the paradigm presented in Kary Oberbrunner's book *Called*. It incorporates the four measurements and components that represent authentic discipleship.

Grace Institute was created out of a strong desire to see theologically trained leaders of all ages who practically incarnate the love of God and others in everyday life. If you desire to know more about Grace Institute please visit: www.karyoberbrunner.com/gi.

# STARVED: *A Parable for the Postmodern World*

Filmed at a buffet restaurant, speaker Kary Oberbrunner takes the viewer on a spiritual journey. Through story-telling he reveals our desperate need to be fed with the Bread of Life every day of the week, not just on Sundays.

**Biblical Texts:** 1 Corinthians 11:18-22; John 4:20-24

**Main Theme:** Until we worship God more than once a week, our spirits will never be satisfied.

**Special Features:** Each video comes with discussion questions for group application.

**Description:** What happens when we're starved? We become impatient, critical, and selfish. All we care about is our own needs and filling our stomachs. Even worse is starving our spirits. When we

.ow up at church, having gone an entire week without feeding our spirits on the True Food and Drink, we set ourselves up for failure. We believe the lie that church is all about us—our needs and preferences. As bingeing and then starving are detrimental to one's physical health so bingeing and then going without spiritual food are damaging to our spirits. Not only do we harm ourselves, but we also hurt the body of Christ. God has a better plan, a balanced plan.

Find out more at KaryOberbrunner.com